Dassault-Breguet Mirage 2000. *M. Keep*

Mirage 2000B

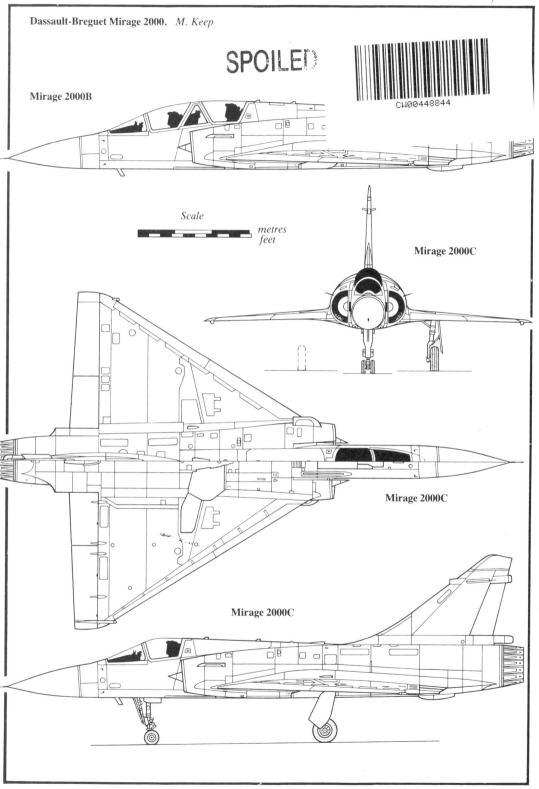

Scale

metres
feet

Mirage 2000C

Mirage 2000C

Mirage 2000C

MIRAGE

Above:
**ECTT 30 at Reims-Champagne was the first wing to
re-equip with Mirage FICs. The wing's two squadrons are
represented here by '30-MP' of ECTT 2/30 'Normandie-
Niemen' and '30-FA' from ECTT 3/30 'Lorraine'.**

Below:
From opposite ends of South America, but brought together in a pre-delivery test flight over France, are a Mirage IIIEA of the Argentine Air Force (top) and a Venezuelan Mirage 5DV.

MIRAGE
Paul Jackson

GUILD PUBLISHING
LONDON

Acknowledgements

Many good friends and colleagues have provided valuable assistance in the preparation of this book, none more so than Jean-Louis Gaynecoetche whose enthusiastic support I acknowledge with gratitude. Comprehensive files made freely available by John Fricker were a constant source of reference, whilst other items of information and elusive photographs were generously contributed by Jean Delmas of the French Branch of Air Britain and the members of AG PHOTO PRESS AERO. The private circulation magazines *Trait d'Union*, *South East Air Review* and *British Aviation Review* were invaluable in positively identifying Mirage exports, and I thank their editors and far-flung correspondents. Others have added to the completeness of this work, but for various reasons must remain anonymous. Three-view drawings of exceptional standard have been prepared by Mike Keep, and I am also grateful to Avions Marcel Dassault-Breguet Aviation for providing other illustrations and diagrams.

Paul Jackson
Bardfield Saling
Essex

First published 1985

This edition published 1985 by Book Club Associates by arrangement with Ian Allan Ltd

Printed in the United Kingdom by Ian Allan Printing Ltd

Contents

1 The Mirage III

Making a Mirage

For a quarter-century the name 'Mirage' has been synonymous with France's top-performance, top-selling fighter aircraft. Forming the backbone of the Armée de l'Air, Mirages have also participated in aerial combat on behalf of some of their many export customers — even fighting under a non de guerre in the Israeli and Argentine air arms. However, it would be wrong to speak of 'The Mirage' as if it were a single type of aircraft, for, as the following pages will show, Mirages come in many shapes and sizes.

Three generations of Mirage are clearly discernible, two of which have scaled-up derivatives optimised for deep penetration missions. Mirages are linked by a common manufacturer and family name — making it logical that they should all find mention in a single volume — but great differences separate the three basic lines.

First came the delta-winged strain epitomised by the Mirage III, 5 and 50, of which some 1,400 have been produced, excluding Israeli Neshers, Daggers and Kfirs. The type, which at the time of writing was still being built — though only in small numbers — formed the basis of the 'big brother' Mirage IV twin-engined strategic nuclear bomber, now being given a new lease of life with stand-off missiles. In the 1970s came the Mirage F1 (around 700 ordered) with its swept wing planform, whilst the current decade has seen a return to the delta, characterised by the Mirage 2000. This too has a larger relation, the as-yet unadopted Mirage 4000, although links with the first generation aircraft are little more than superficial because of the immense advances attained in the fields of aerodynamics and avionics in the intervening years.

Below:
The first public showing of an export Mirage 2000 took place at the 1985 Paris Salon when Peruvian 2000DP No 193 appeared in the static display, wearing a brown and sand camouflage scheme, but without national insignia.

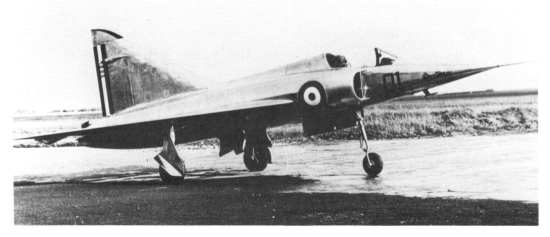

Above:
Mirage Genesis: The Dassault MD.550 had but a superficial resemblance to later Mirages. The sole aircraft is seen in this rare photograph to be wearing the original name 'Mystère' followed by the Greek letter, delta.

The Mirage story starts, modestly enough, with a dumpy little delta which bore another name when it made its initial flight during 1955. To place the aircraft in historical perspective, however, it is necessary to return to World War 2 and its aftermath.

During the five years of German occupation, the French aircraft industry had been relegated to the inferior status of sub-contractor for the Luftwaffe, its previous design expertise dissipated. This was a severe blow to a country which had once been in the forefront of aeronautical development, and there was thus strong determination to make up for lost time. World progress in aviation had been spurred considerably by the war, making the task even more formidable.

The nationalised aircraft industry re-emerged — as did the independent firm of Marcel Bloch, which became Marcel Dassault, the name taken by the founder's brother during his time as a Resistance leader (from Char *d'Assaut*: battle tank). Whilst the Armée de l'Air (AA) flew high-performance aircraft from Britain and the USA — building its own de Havilland Vampires as the 'Mistral' — local industry designed a plethora of experimental machines. The unkind observer may have concluded that France was determined not to make a conventional-looking aircraft where one of grotesque appearance could be produced, yet the numerous journeys to and beyond the limits of aeronautical knowledge paid dividends.

Sociétés de Avions (later Générale Aéronautique) Marcel Dassault had progressed sufficiently for the AA to place its straight-winged Ouragan in service during 1952. This was the first indigenous jet to take its place in a fighter squadron, but it soon gave way to a swept version known as the Mystère II and its more refined development, the Mystère IV.

In 1953 — a year before the subsonic Mystère IV took its place in the front line — the AA requested proposals from industry in response to a specification for a light fighter. Drawing on the lessons of air combat in Korea, the requirement placed emphasis on supersonic speed *and* its rapid attainment, the preferred solution being a combination of turbojet and rocket power. What was wanted was the smallest possible interceptor capable of reaching 60,000ft in six minutes, carrying all-weather armament.

Four aircraft companies rose to the challenge, including Sud-Est with its SE.212 Durandal employing (prophetically) an afterburning SNECMA Atar, plus a SEPR 65 liquid-propellant rocket produced by Société d'Étude de la Propulsion par Réaction. Sud-Ouest offered the SO.9050 Trident II derived from the SO.9000 research airicraft, this having an Armstrong-Siddeley Viper in wingtip pods and a SEPR 631 rocket in the slim fuselage. Unlike its competitor (and stable-mate from March 1957 when Sud-Est and Sud-Ouest combined to form Sud-Aviation), the Trident classified its rocket as the main propulsor, this serving to highlight the dangers of such power when inadvertent and catastrophic mixture of the self-igniting furaline and nitric acid fuels destroyed one of the prototypes in flight during May 1957.

Like Sud-Est, Dassault opted for a detachable rocket pack which could be refuelled away from the aircraft, and this was not fitted for early flights of the company's light fighter submission, the MD.550. Both Dassault and Sud-Est fighters were deltas, as was Nord's 1500 Griffon, powered by an Atar plus one of the manufacturer's own ramjets. At one time Nord might have been imagined to have the lead over its rivals, for on 3 August 1954 the N.1302 Gerfaut had become the first aircraft to exceed Mach 1 in level flight without afterburner or ramjet assistance.

Having acquired a licence for Viper manufacture from Armstrong-Siddeley Motors Ltd in 1953, Dassault employed two of these powerplants — designated MD.30 — in the MD.550. Each engine produced 1,753lb (795kg) of thrust, whilst the intended SEPR 66 rocket would later almost double this by contributing a further 3,300lb (1,500kg).

Initially, the MD.550 was known as the 'Mystère Delta', and as such it first flew at Melun-Villaroche in the hands of Roland Glavany on 25 June 1955. The legend 'Mystère' was applied to the nose, followed by the triangular shape of a Greek letter delta, this changing to 'Mirage' early in the trials programme, and ultimately to 'Mirage I'. Ahead of the intakes was the aircraft identity '01' — largely superfluous as the planned second prototype was not completed.

Limited at first by low engine power, the aircraft could only reach Mach 1.15 in a shallow dive. Modifications ensued, including fitment of a Dassault afterburner to boost the re-designated MD.30R turbojet to 2,160lb (980kg), reduction of wing span by 0.27m (10.5in) from 7.32m (24ft 0in), and addition of the SEPR rocket and associated small dorsal fin. Thus transformed, the Mirage I used its sources of additional power for the first time on 17 December 1956, achieving Mach 1.3 in level flight.

Development of the Mirage continued at Dassault's St Cloud (Paris) premises, largely outside the public gaze. (Indeed, it is interesting to note — particularly in view of the current trend for large-scale publicity of even design office schemes — that the 1955-56 issue of that erstwhile authority, *Jane's All the World's Aircraft*, could only summon-up a meagre 63 words on the MD.550.) It was realised, however, that with a loaded weight of 5,400kg (11,905lb) the Mirage I was impractically small for an all-weather fighter, and like the British parallel, the Folland Gnat, its raison d'être was discredited and discarded.

Fortunately, Dassault already had a larger, more suitable aircraft on the drawing board, the MD.550 having acted as a proof vehicle for its tailless delta configuration. In the Mirage II, power was to be provided by two Turbomeca Gabizo turbojets, each of 1,090kg (2,400lb) thrust — 1,500kg (3,310lb) with reheat — and a pair of rockets contributing 750kg (1,650lb) apiece. Estimates revealed that the Mirage II could attain Mach 1.55 at 36,000ft: better, but not good enough for an Air Staff requiring Mach 2.

By another stroke of good fortune, the Mirage II was overtaken by events. More information on high-speed delta aerofoils came in from Britain's Fairey Delta 2 programme, whilst talk across the Atlantic was of a new theory known as 'area rule', the application of which would dramatically improve the aerodynamic efficiency of aircraft intended to pass beyond the speed of sound. Additionally, Dassault was planning production of an R-70 version of the ASV.10 Viper with dry power equivalent to the Gabizo, and naturally wished to use two company-built engines wherever possible, instead of the Turbomeca product.

All these features demanded incorporation in the projected aircraft, and such was their radical effect on the design that a new name was appropriate: France's next-generation fighter was to be known as the Mirage III.

Below:
Roland Glavany piloted the Mirage Delta on its maiden flight from Melun-Villaroche on 25 June 1955, the disproportionately large fin being clearly evident in this view.

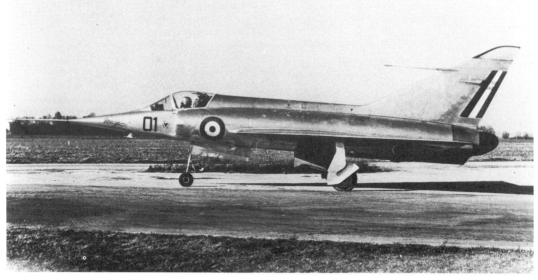

After modification, the MD.550 prototype appeared with a revised fin mounting a second pitot, and the name 'Mirage' on the nose. The fate of this historic aircraft is not recorded, but it was almost certainly broken up.

Transformation of the Mystère Delta into a combat-ready Mirage III was a complex process achieved in a commendably short time by a small staff. Chapters could be written on company design philosophy, but the whole is neatly summed-up in a set of three cartoons held by Marcel Dassault to be his favourites. The first is a caricature of US design methods and shows bank upon bank of computers attended by hosts of programmers feeding-in reams of analyses. Next is the Soviet method of producing aircraft: an immense pool of labour being spurred on by a people's commissar. In the third drawing a newly rolled-out aircraft is having its health drunk by just three men, one of whom — apparently the principal figure — is wearing an artist's smock. That is the Dassault way.

Of the last-minute brush-strokes required by the emergent Mirage III, the most drastic was a complete revision of the powerplant. A single engine was selected to replace the two units of all earlier schemes, choice falling on the SNECMA Atar. The basis of this turbojet was the German

BMW-012, although considerable development had been undertaken in France by Société Nationale d'Étude et de Construction de Moteurs d'Aviation (SNECMA). ('Atar' indicated Atelier Technique Aéronautique Reichenbach, rather than the town of that name in French West Africa.)

Powered by an Atar 101G-1 of 4,500kg (9,920lb) thrust, aided by a single SEPR 66 rocket, the Mirage III-001 prototype was built by a comparatively small staff of 62 and readied for its maiden flight at Villaroche. Larger and heavier than the Mirage I, with a new area-ruled fuselage profile and leading edge sweepback increased from 55° to 60°, it nevertheless continued to bear the MD.550 designation.

Below:
The Mirage III clearly owed a lot to the Dassault MD.550, as seen when it appeared late in 1956. Its early flights were made without the rocket motor installed.

Mirage I-III Prototypes

Aircraft	First flight/pilot	Remarks
Mirage I	25 June 1955 R. Glavany	Withdrawn 1958 and used for fire trials at Villaroche.
III-001	17 November 1956 R.Glavany	Converted to Balzac V.
IIIA-01	12 May 1958 R. Glavany	Last flown by F. Cousson at CEV, Bretigny, 11 May 1966. Used for taxying trials until 8 May 1972. Preserved at Musée de l'Air, Le Bourget
IIIA-02	17 February 1959 R. Glavany	CEV: Atar 09 and SEPR rocket trials. Armée de l'Air static exhibit. Preserved at ENSAE, Toulouse.
IIIA-03	28 March 1959 R. Glavany	Performance and engine trials. First IIIA evaluated by CEAM. Transferred to EPNER. Crashed on landing at Istres 28 October 1968 — pilot (A. Brossier) ejected safely.
IIIA-04	7 May 1959 J. M. Saget	Equipment trials. Last flight 28 February 1975 (pilot: A Hisler) at Brétigny. Scrapped.
IIIA-05	10 May 1959 R. Glavany	Production standard airframe. Performance comparison trials. Crashed during demonstration flight at Bretigny, 13 October 1960 (J. Blankaert killed).
IIIA-06	11 July 1959 R. Glavany	Nosecone trials. Radar trials. Preliminary trials for Mirage IIIE. Last flown at Bretigny (pilot Boiter) 11 January 1974. Preserved at Dassault-Breguet, Biarritz.
IIIA-07	10 November 1959 R. Bigand	CEAM: Braking parachute. CEV. Swiss evaluation. Transferred to EPNER. Withdrawn from use.
IIIA-08	22 July 1959 J. M. Saget	CEV: First with Cyrano Ibis. Armament trials: MATRA R.511, R.530, Nord AS.20, AS.30, DEFA cannon. Last flown at Brétigny, 28 February 1975 (pilot Chautemps). Mobile recruiting display.
IIIA-09	9 September 1959 R. Bigand	Armament trials. Damaged by Swiss pilot. Repaired. Crashed at Cazaux 20 June 1961. Used for arrestor barrier trials.
IIIA-10	15 December 1959 Buge	CEAM evaluation. SNECMA for Atar 9K50 engine trials. Returned to CEV, Istres

Notes

All first flights made at Melun-Villaroche.
CEV: Centre d'Essais en Vol, Brétigny, Cazaux and Istres.
CEAM: Centre d'Expérimentations Aériennes Militaires, Mont-de-Marsan.
EPNER: École du Personel Navigant d'Essais et de Réception.

Above:
Equipped with an SEPR rocket motor beneath the rear fuselage, the Mirage III prototype achieved Mach 1.52 on its 10th flight, on 30 January 1957.

Below:
The well-known lines of the first-generation Mirage had been established by the time the Mirage IIIA appeared in May 1958. Prototype IIIA-01 retained the fin pitot for its early trials.

11

Roland Glavany was again the pilot when No 001 was first airborne on 17 November 1956, limiting his speed to 700km/hr (377mph) in the course of a sortie lasting some 40 minutes. Within a month, sufficient experience had been gained for the rocket motor to be installed (it was jettisonable as a safety measure in the event of a crash and could be replaced by a fuel tank). Test pilot Gerard Muselli tried the rocket on 17 December, whilst during the 10th flight, on 30 January 1957, Glavany used reheat and rocket to achieve the aircraft's maximum level speed of Mach 1.52 at 38,000ft, then entered a 20° dive to increase this to Mach 1.60. Naturally, the rocket provided additional speed, although its principal function was to increase the aircraft's ceiling.

As a prototype, No 001 was subjected to numerous modifications, one of the more important being the addition of manually-operated half-cone centre-bodies in the air intakes. (These rapidly gained the name — which has stuck — of 'souris': mouse.) Resembling the fixed units on the Lockheed Starfighter, these moved fore or aft at faster and slower speeds to focus the resultant shock wave in the optimum position on the intake lip for pressure recovery, and to exclude the unstable flow, or 'buzz', from the duct.

The modification had the effect of increasing thrust by almost 20%, and in conjunction with a newly-installed 4,400kg (9,700lb) thrust after-burning Atar 101G-2, it allowed the aircraft to demonstrate a speed of Mach 1.65 on 17 April 1958 — more than could be attained with the rocket in the previous configuration. With the SEPR 66 in operation, maximum speed was Mach 1.80.

In its revised form the aircraft was evaluated by West Germany's Luftwaffe in an assessment programme which eventually led to purchase of Lockheed Starfighters. Part of the reason for the Mirage being passed over was that French emphasis was on interception (even within Dassault) and Germany wanted multi-role capability, but the Luftwaffe was unable to judge the full potential of the aircraft because development of its radar and fire-control systems were far behind the airframe. Indeed, the projected Dassault equipment for the Mirage was cancelled at a time when the substitute CSF Cyrano was still in the development stage.

The most far-reaching result of the unproductive German trials was a realisation that the Mirage

Below:
Trials from a semi-prepared airfield were conducted by Mirage IIIA-01 after its flight to twice the speed of sound in October 1958 — hence the 'Mach 2' legend applied to the nose.

could — and should — be a multi-role aircraft. Design included provision for take-offs from short or semi-prepared airstrips, and with the addition of other appropriate equipment there was no reason why the aircraft could not become a useful support for land forces. (One of the more drastic short take-off schemes considered was launching the aircraft from a ramp similar to that employed for the Martin Matador missile — 4g acceleration being provided by two rockets giving 13,000kg (28,660lb) of thrust for 2.5sec. Perhaps to the relief of many, this idea did not proceed.)

Despite delays with its avionics, the Mirage was clearly the most promising prototype fighter in France, and officialdom apparently agreed when it placed an order for 10 development models, to be designated Mirage IIIA. Once more, opportunity was taken to revise the design, and in the IIIA wing area increased from 29 to 34sq m (312 to 366sq ft), whilst to offset the additional drag this caused, thickness/chord ratio fell from 5% to 4.5% at the root and 3.5% at the tip. Following trials with III-001, conical camber was subsequently added to the leading edge and chordwise incisions made to perform the function of wing fences. As a result the outer elevon sections assumed a promiment downward curve, and wing area went up to 34.85sq m (375sq ft).

Atar development had now reached the 09B of 6,000kg (13,225lb) thrust (with reheat), and a longer fuselage was introduced to accommodate the much improved engine with its additional compressor and turbine stages. Further rocket power was also on hand, and so the IIIAs used a SEPR 841 unit which could provide 680kg (1,500lb) of thrust for 160sec or 1,360kg (3,000lb) for 80sec.

Mirage IIIA-001 was airborne from Villaroche on 12 May 1958 with Roland Glavany in command, the remaining nine aircraft all following during 1959. Each was allocated a development task, one of the more significant being No 05 (flown on 10 May 1959) which was to production standard, including the plastic nose radome and its balancing ventral fin. The definitive Cyrano Ibis radar was not installed until No 08, however, and aircraft from IIIA-01 carried the Dassault Aida unit, as fitted to the company's Etendard.

No 01 also had its claim to fame, becoming the first French aircraft to reach Mach 2 without rocket assistance. Flown from Istres by Glavany, it achieved its feat on 24 October 1958 — just a month before another Roland (Beamont) took Britain's English Electric Lightning to that speed. Showing no sexual discrimination, No 01 was made available for Jacqueline Auriol to become the first Mach 2 female on 26 August 1959.

Trials with the 10 development aircraft confirmed the Mirage III to be highly effective in both interception and ground attack roles. Aerodynamically it was almost right from the start, changes being restricted to the leading-edge camber mentioned earlier and an extension of the dorsal fin. As innumerable combinations of air-to-air and air-surface missiles, bombs, rockets and fuel tanks were tested and approved for service, Dassault tooled-up and prepared factory space for the large orders which would inevitably follow.

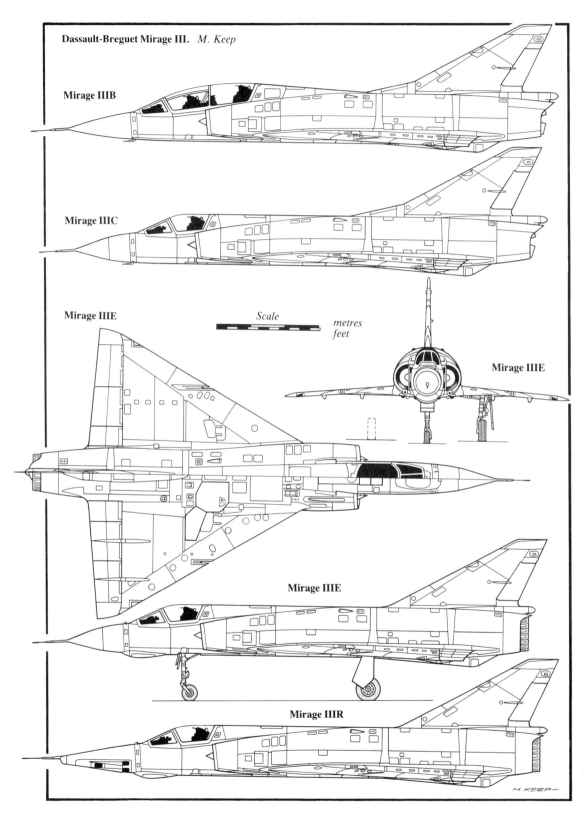

Dassault-Breguet Mirage III. *M. Keep*

Mirage IIIB

Mirage IIIC

Mirage IIIE

Scale

metres
feet

Mirage IIIE

Mirage IIIE

Mirage IIIE

Mirage IIIR

M. KEEP

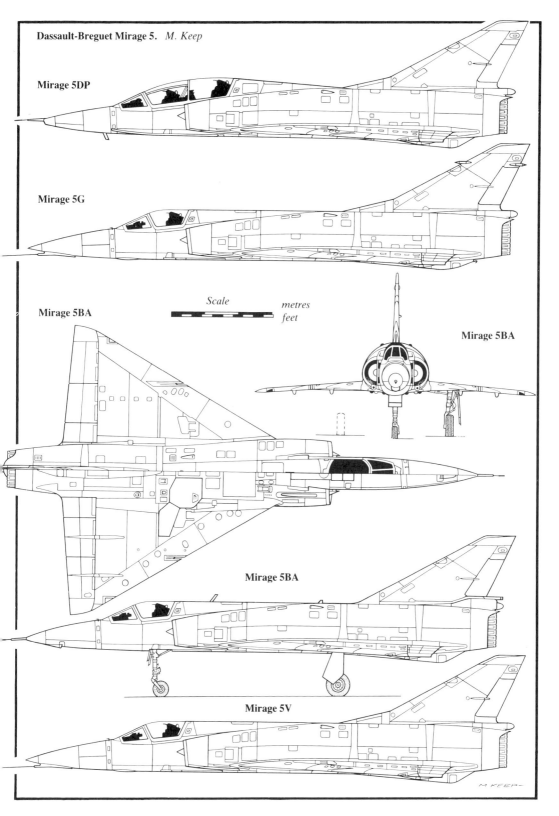

Dassault-Breguet Mirage 5. *M. Keep*

Mirage 5DP

Mirage 5G

Mirage 5BA

Scale

metres
feet

Mirage 5BA

Mirage 5BA

Mirage 5V

M KEEP-

15

Above:
Mirage IIIA-07 (note the revised fin shape) first flew in November 1959 and participated in Swiss trials which led to an early export order. It ended its service career with the French test pilots' school, EPNER.

Below:
Variants of the CSF Cyrano radar have been associated with the Mirage family since the earliest days of production. A Cyrano II in the nose of a Mirage IIIC is here on view, its radome mounted in a mobile cradle.

Production and Construction

Such was the eventual magnitude of the Mirage III manufacturing effort that Dassault was, in the late-1970s, producing only 14% by value of the aircraft, with the remainder coming from sub-contractors. The company had always placed considerable reliance on outside assistance, but offset agreements granted to Mirage purchasers diversified the fabrication process even further. The parent firm itself gained additional production capacity in December 1971 when it merged with Breguet Aviation, and Dassault-Breguet currently carries out its widespread activities in plants at Saint Cloud, Melun-Villaroche, Argenteuil, Boulogne/Seine, Velizy-Villacoublay, Martignas, Bordeaux-Mérignac, Bretigny, Cazaux, Toulouse-Colomiers, Biarritz-Parme (Anglet), Istres, Argonay, Le Bourget, Lille-Seclin and Poitiers.

In the case of the first-generation Mirage, the main centres were Argenteuil (a suburb of Paris), where fuselage assembly is undertaken, and Bordeaux-Mérignac, the final assembly and flight-test centre which combined fins built at Talence and the wings sub-contracted to Nord at Meaulte.

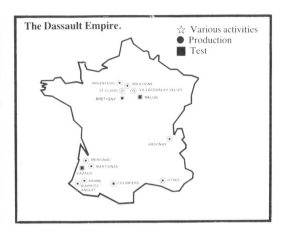

Below:
Dassault's Mirage III assembly line at Bordeaux-Mérignac was heavily reliant on sub-contracted components by the late-1970s, with the parent firm producing only 14% by value of the completed aircraft. A Mirage 5 trainer is in the foreground, with the Mirage F1 line behind.

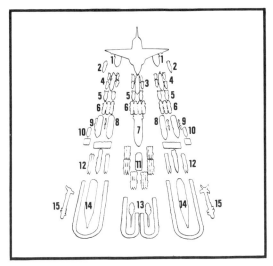

Left:
The wide range of armament options has been a feature of the Mirage's success in the international market. For the Mirage 5 this includes: 1 — two 1,700litre tanks (attached to aircraft); 2 — two 500litre tanks; 3 — launcher for four 250kg bombs; 4 — two RPK bomb launchers; 5 — six 400kg bombs; 6 — 10 Durandal anti-runway bombs; 7 — 1,300litre tank; 8 — two JL100 rocket launchers (18×68mm rockets, plus 250litre tank); 9 — two CEM.1 multi-store adaptors (18×68mm, plus four practice bombs); 10 — two F2 rocket launchers (6×68mm); 11 — 18 BAT100 anti-runway bombs; 12 — two C4 rocket launchers (4×100mm); 13 — two DEFA 552 30mm cannon (internal) with 125 rounds each; 14 — two CC420 30mm gun pods with 250 rounds each; and 15 — two MATRA R.550 Magic AAMs.

Below:
In addition to the SEPR rocket, the Mirage III may use JATO bottles for short take-offs. Such an ability is of value to the Swiss Air Force, whose first Mirage IIIS is pictured undergoing trials at Bordeaux.

All the Dassault facilities have recently become the property of the French State in a gradual nationalisation programme, beginning with the taking of a 20% stake in January 1979. The Government's holding increased to 46% in November 1981, and as some of its shares carry double voting rights, this was sufficient to secure control of the company. One of Dassault's most significant achievements had been to produce combat aircraft with greater operational and sales potential than those of the nationalised sector of the French aircraft industry. It must therefore have been a source of wry amusement to the aged but still active founder of the company that the State had to resort to legislation to gain control of the aircraft family which had done so much for France's pride and its balance of payments.

One of the many success-making aspects of the Mirage III was its ease of construction. today it is almost axiomatic that an aeroplane cannot be better than its rivals without use of some advanced technology. With the mirage, however, Dassault set out to produce a better aeroplane with only the materials and techniques already current in Europe — and having done so, the rewards were great.

The Mirage IIIE, major production variant for the Armée de l'Air, best represents the Mirage III series and has a majority of features in common with the later Mirage 5 and 50. Its basis is an all-metal fuselage built in seven segments, each fabricated in halves, and 'waisted' to conform with area rule. The cockpit shows all the signs of being carefully designed for ease of operation, and

contains a single Hispano-built Martin-Baker RM.4 zero-altitude ejection seat beneath a rear-hinged canopy. In spite of the restricted space available, the layout is logical thanks to miniaturisation of all indicators except the main flight instruments and radar scope.

Cantilever low-mounted delta wings, incorporating conical camber, are without incidence and have a thickness/chord ratio diminishing from 4.5% to 3.5% at the tips. Aspect ratio is 1.94, and anhedral 1°. Leading edge sweepback is 60° 34'. Wings are of all-metal, torsion box structure, with a stressed skin of machined panels having integral stiffeners. The elevons are hydraulically powered — at 210kg/sq cm (3,000lb/sq in) pressure — featuring artificial 'feel' pioneeeed by Dassault. The Mirage's air brakes are mounted in the wings, taking the form of hinged panels, above and below.

Various styles of fin, with and without fillets, will be seen on Mirages, all having a cantilever construction and a hydraulically-powered rudder — with Dassault artificial 'feel'. The undercarriage is of the usual tricycle type for jet aircraft and retracts hydraulically, main wheels inwards, nose wheel rearwards. Mainwheel tyre pressure is between 6 and 10kg/sq cm (85.5 to 142lb/sq in), and hydraulic disc brakes are backed up by a parachute.

Power for the Mirage IIIE is provided by a SNECMA Atar 09C turbojet of 6,200kg (13,670lb) afterburning thrust, which is fitted with an overspeed system engaged automatically from March 1.4 to provide a thrust increase of some 8% in the high supersonic speed range. The jettisonable rocket motor in the rear fuselage is a SEPR 884 of 1,500kg (3,300lb) thrust, although this can be exchanged in 20 minutes for a fuel tank to increase total internal capacity to 3,330litre (733Imp gal). Further fuel may be carried in a pair of drop-tanks beneath the wings, each containing 600, 1,300 or 1,700litre (132, 285 or 374Imp gal).

Heading the aircraft's combat systems (in more senses than one) is the nose-mounted Cyrano II fire control radar, produced by Compagnie générale de télégraphie Sans Fil (CSF) to an official specification, and adopted by many of the Mirage's export customers. In addition to the expected air-air mode for interception, Cyrano II can be employed to give a radar picture of major ground features for high-level navigation; to display all obstacles above a pre-selected height when low flying or making a blind descent; and to measure oblique distances between aircraft and a ground point. The last-mentioned data is displayed in the complementary CSF 97 sight, which provides an air-air mode for missiles or cannon; air-ground for dive-bombing or LABS; and a navigational facility to indicate heading and horizon.

For its day, the Mirage had a sophisticated automatic navigation system which constantly presents heading and distance of the target and includes a rotating magazine holding up to 12 plastic punch-cards — each representing the co-ordinates of a position. Navigational data is provided for the pilot to take appropriate manual action as he flies the pre-selected path derived from the cards, additional lattitude being provided by the ability to nominate unplanned way-points in flight. Ground-speed and drift information for navigation is supplied by Marconi Doppler equipment mounted in a blister beneath the forward fuselage, and bearings and distances to TACAN beacons are shown on the instrument panel.

Intercept missions are flown with the normal internal armament of two 30mm DEFA cannon (125 rounds per gun) and an AAM fit comprising a single MATRA R.530 semi-active radar or infra-red missile on the centre pylon and/or a pair of IR weapons beneath the wings. The US-produced AIM-9 Sidewinder was previously used in the latter connection, but has given way to the MATRA R.550 Magic. The reader will doubtless be familiar with publicity photographs showing a Mirage standing before an array of air-ground

Below:
The blunted nose and repositioned pitot is a recognition feature of the Mirage IIIR reconnaissance model, based on a Mirage IIIE airframe. The prototype, pictured here, first flew in October 1961.

Early production Mirage IIIR No 307 reveals the arrangement of cameras in the nose and an inscription to identify it as the aircraft in which Jacqueline Auriol broke the women's 100km closed-circuit record on 14 June 1963.

weaponry options seemingly occupying several acres. Suffice to record, therefore, that up to 4,000kg (8,820lb) of ordinance (or fuel) can be carried on five external hardpoints, principal items including an Aérospatiale AS.30 ASM (centreline position), 1,000lb (454kg) bombs, and JL-100 pods which combine 18 rockets with 250litre (55Imp gal) of fuel.

Flying the tail-less delta Mirage presents few problems to the competent pilot, except that he will have to learn a new technique for that most critical phase, the landing, if he has not flown an aircraft with such a configuration before. Take-off though is little different from any other jet fighter, and with afterburner on it involves lifting the non-steerable nosewheel at 110kt (204km/hr) and an 'unstick' at around 155kt (287km/hr) using a slightly more nose-up attitude than normal. Undercarriage retraction must be before passing 220kt (408km/hr), although the gear is cleared to 250kt (463km/hr) for extension and 270kt (500km/hr) when locked down.

Pilots without delta experience need to take care during the early stages of Mirage III conversion because angle of attack becomes a dominant factor when the narrow delta is flying below about 240kt (445km/hr), and a small increase in angle will considerably boost the drag. In its landing approach the Mirage III is well 'on the back of the drag curve', where increased speed can only be provided by a vast amount of power, and if a pilot attempts to adjust his attitude in the 'normal' manner he can find himself producing sink, rather than speed. In addition, the Mirage III passes 'over the fence' at a fairly brisk rate, approaching at 183kt (340km/hr) and landing at 157kt (290km/hr). This may be contrasted with the more

docile 129.5kt (240km/hr) approach speed of the contemporary McDonnell F-4B Phanton although, to be fair, a modest landing speed is higher on the list of priorities for a naval fighter.

If the foregoing creates the impression that the Mirage III can be temperamental on the approach, it should be recalled that from the earliest days of its service with the Armée de l'Air, pilots regularly practised dead-stick landings. Starting from 15,000ft above the airfield and using air brakes to negate residual thrust from the idling engine, the procedure is to descend at some 240kt (445km/hr) and 7,000ft/min (35.5m/sec) before flaring-out well short of the ground and killing any excess speed with the wing planform on the round-out. At the time, such training on a delta was unique.

In the early-1960s prospective Mirage pilots were required to have a modest 300 hours in their logbooks: 200 on the Magister and T-33, plus 100 flying the Mystère IVA. After simulator training and sorties in a two-seat Mirage IIIB, covering the flight envelope up to March 1.8, about a dozen flights in a IIIC were sufficient to complete the airframe conversion totalling 35 flights in three months. The full course was 100 sorties in six months, with the balance dedicated to weapons techniques, operating of the Cyrano radar and all-weather conversion. This achieved, the next step was a place in one of the growing number of French combat squadrons using the Mirage for interception, ground attack and reconnaissance.

Above:
In typical landing posture with parachute deployed is a Mirage IIIC assigned to development duties.

Less than three months' flying had been accumulated by the first of the 10 development Mirage IIIAs before the Armée de l'Air (AA) demonstrated its faith in the design by placing, on 5 August 1958, a FF60,000million contract for 100 aircraft. Initial manufacture was to be of the Mirage IIIC single-seat all-weather interceptor and day ground-attack fighter, the first of which flew from Bordeaux-Mérignac on 9 October 1960, piloted by Jean Coreau. Within a year Dassault was turning out Mirages at the rate of nine per month.

France's premier fighter wing, the 2nd, was chosen to introduce the new aircraft to operational service, and early in 1961 its first pilots discarded their Mystère IVAs and reported to the CEAM at Mont-de-Marsan for a Mirage conversion course. Re-equipment proper started on 10 July 1961 when Mirage IIIC No 23 was delivered to the 2 Wing base at Dijon-Longvic and decorated on the fin with the stork insignia of the first squadron and the code letters 2-EA.

The French method of identifying squadrons and perpetuating their traditions is somewhat complex, and therefore a few words of explanation may be of value (see also Appendix 2). The historical identity of a squadron, or escadron, comprises a name (usually that of a region of France) and, in most cases, the badges of two component flights (escadrilles) — the latter related to World War 1 squadrons — applied to opposite sides of the fin. The position number of a squadron within a wing, or Escadron, is not fixed, and will in any case change when squadrons are transferred to other wings. The code group, worn on the nose or centre fuselage, is a combination of the wing number and the aircraft's radio call-sign, the final letter running from A to Z within each squadron.

The first Mirage unit was Escadron de Chasse (EC — Fighter Squadron) 1/2 'Cigognes', whose component flights were escadrilles SPA 3 and SPA 103.

After an early accident, resulting in the loss of No 29 on 23 August and grounding of the Mirage IIIC from then until 6 September, EC 1/2 reached its outhorised strength of 15 aircraft in December and completed 10,000 hours on the type in September 1965. Also in December 1961, the first IIIC for the other component of 2e Escadre, EC 3/2 'Alsace', arrived at Dijon. The missing EC 2/2 allocation was not filled until April 1965 when 'Côte d'Or' squadron formed as the Mirage III operational conversion unit, its duties subsequently including training of pilots for Mirage purchasers as diverse as Spain, Libya, Argentina, Saudi Arabia and Zaire.

Below:
Escadron de Chasse 1/2 'Cigognes', based at Dijon-Longvic, was the first squadron equipped with Mirage IIICs, deliveries beginning in July 1961.

Naturally the conversion unit's equipment included the two-seat Mirage IIIB, first flown in prototype form on 20 October 1959. An equivalent to the IIIC, the trainer is longer in order to accommodate a second seat beneath an extended rear-hinged canopy, and lacks radar and cannon, although two 30mm DEFA weapons can be installed if the rear seat is temporarily removed. Numbered '201', the first production IIIB flew on 19 July 1962 and those which followed were issued to Mirage III squadrons until brought together within EC 2/2, or the nuclear strike force training unit, Centre d'Instruction des Forces Aériennes Stratégiques (CIFAS), at Bordeaux-Mérignac.

By November 1964 Dassault had completed the 95th and last Mirage IIIC for the AA, allowing EC 13 to convert from F-86K Sabres at Colmar. No 56 was delivered to EC 1/13 'Artois' on 13 March 1962, and conversion of EC 2/13 'Alpes' began with the arrival of No 73 on 29 May, but three years later the wing moved up to the Mirage IIIE, and the surplus IIICs allowed EC 5 to trade in its Super Mystère B2s at Orange.

Above:
Late in their careers, some of the remaining Mirage IIICs of EC 2/10 'Seine' changed from natural metal to overall light blue 'air superiority' colours.

Below:
Destined to be the final Mirage IIIC unit, EC 3/10 'Vexin' is based at Djibouti, East Africa. Its aircraft wear a unique camouflage scheme of 'sand and chestnut'.

Until recently, however, only EC 10 operated the IIIC, having first equipped EC 1/10 'Valois' in December 1968, followed by EC 2/10 'Seine' in August 1974 and EC 3/10 'Vexin' in January 1979. Mirage Fls took over in the first squadron in 1981 and EC 2/10 disbanded in 1985, although the third component was not based at Creil with the wing HQ, but in the Horn of Africa. 'Vexin', with 10 Mirage IIICs marked in a unique sand and chestnut camouflage scheme, provides an air defence and attack force for the former French colony of Djibouti against the territorial ambitions of Somalia, demonstrating that the ageing first production model can still be trusted with an operational assignment.

The IIIB trainer, too, remains active. AA acquired 26 of the initial model for regular conversion duties, of which No 225 was passed to the CEV for variable stability experiments as the Mirage IIIB-SV. There followed five IIIB-1 testbeds for a variety of programmes at the CEV, and then 10 IIIB-RVs. 'RV' indicates Ravitaillement en Vol, or in-flight refuelling, and these aircraft, delivered between July 1967 and October 1968, are fitted with training IFR probes for use by the CIFAS. Finally, contracts were placed for an eventual total of 20 IIIBE models, produced from February 1971 onwards and compatible with the Mirage IIIE in terms of equipment and an Atar 09C-3 turbojet. They all went to the OCU, which as Escadron de Chasse et de Transformation 2/2, added a third flight from October 1972 to accommodate the larger complement. In conse-

quence its aircraft now display considerable variation of fin markings, comprising permutations of the three squadron insignia.

After the Mirage IIIB and IIIC, the next stage in development of the design for home use was represented by the IIIE tactical nuclear strike and ground attack model and the IIIR tactical reconnaissance version. Externally, these differ from their single-seat predecessor in having a 30cm (11.8in) fuselage extension which moves the bottom edge of the cockpit canopy completely forward of the air intakes (the recce aircraft is even longer because of its modified camera nose), under-carriage legs raked forward to give clearance for an AN52 nuclear weapon or large drop-tank, and a revised fin shape omitting the forward extension.

Three Mirage IIIE prototypes were produced, No 01 flying on 5 April 1961, and there were also two trials aircraft for the IIIR, of which No 01 first flew on 31 October the same year. With the IIIC's navigation system and air-ground weapons capability, the IIIR was able to enter service well before its strike-configured predecessor, first production aircraft (No 301) taking to the air on 1 February

Below:
Distinctive features of the Mirage IIIE, as modelled by the prototype, include a fin lacking the fillet, and a longer fuselage (the air intakes being in line with the rear of the cockpit). However, IIIE-01 lacks the Doppler fitment ahead of the nosewheel.

1963. Contracts covered 50 IIIRs produced up to March 1965 and 20 IIIRDs completed between July 1967 and January 1969. Both have a fan of five OMERA 31 optical cameras replacing the radar and capable of being focused in four different arrangements for ultra-low, medium, high and night missions, but the IIIRD is also equipped with an improved Doppler navigation system in an

Top left:
The first production Mirage IIIE took to the air in January 1964, and has now completed 21 years of service.

Centre left:
Deliveries of production Mirage IIIEs were first made to EC 2/13 'Alpes' at Colmar in 1965, replacing Mirage IIICs. The squadron's flamboyant fin insignia is readily apparent.

Left:
An unusual photograph of a Mirage IIIE taking off on a target-towing sortie, showing the drogue temporarily mounted below the starboard wingtip and a cable drum pod on the centre line.

Above:
At Mont-de-Marsan, the trials establishment, CEAM operates a small fleet of development Mirages. An Aérospatiale (Nord) AS 30 air-to-surface missile is being carried on the centre pylon of Mirage IIIE No 506.

under-fuselage blister fairing, gyro gunsight, automatic camera control and has provision for SAT Cyclope infra-red tracking equipment in a ventral fairing.

France has only one specialist tactical recce wing — 33e Escadre de Reconnaissance — and that unit's ER 3/33 'Moselle' received its first IIIR at Strasbourg on 7 June 1963 after crew training with the CEAM. Mirages replaced the wing's Republic RF-84F Thunderflashes gradually, for although ER 2/33 'Savoie' converted from January 1964 onwards, three years elapsed before ER 1/33 'Belfort' began to follow suit. The first two squadrons were able to increase their strengths when ER 3/33 converted to new IIIRDs from April 1968.

Left:
Mirage IIIEs, in grey and green camouflage, still had an air defence commitment with EC 3/2 'Alsace' at Dijon in 1984. Beneath the fuselage of this example is a MATRA R.530E radar-guided AAM.

Centre left:
Only in their earliest days were Mirage IIIB two-seat trainers flown by units other than the OCU. Markings on this aircraft are of reconnaissance squadron ER 2/33 'Savoie' at Strasbourg.

Bottom left:
Despite having had its nose put out of joint in this mishap, Mirage IIIB No 209 continues to serve with ECT 2/2 'Côte d'Or' at Dijon.

Bottom:
In recent years even Mirage IIIB trainers have adopted a coat of camouflage, modelled here by No 206 of ECT 2/2.

Time has begun to run out for the IIIR, as evidenced by the conversion of ER 2/33 to Mirage F1CRs during 1983, followed by ER 1/33 in 1985. Because of funding difficulties, there may not be sufficient F1CRs for ER 3/33, so its ageing IIIRDs might have to soldier on for a little while longer. Spare IIIRs have been held in reserve at Strasbourg, although four had their cameras removed before transferring to ECT 2/2 in May 1983 for use in the advanced stage of Mirage III type conversion.

Meanwhile, Mirage IIIE production was getting into its stride with the maiden flight of No 401 on 14 January 1964. Four wings rapidly took up the aircraft, beginning with Colmar-based EC 13, which received its first (No 417 '13-PA') on 1 April 1965 as a replacement for Mirage IIICs in the strike/attack and interception roles. At Lahr, West Germany, personnel formerly flying North American F-100 Super Sabres with EC 3 started Mirage conversion at Colmar on 15 September 1965 prior to the first aircraft for the wing's EC 2/3 'Champagne' arriving there on 17 January next. Full operational status was achieved at Lahr in July 1967, just two months before the wing moved to Nancy as the result of France's withdrawal from the military side of NATO; the wing was later to adopt the defence-suppression role using the MATRA/HS AJ37 MARTEL (Missile Anti-Radar et Télévision).

Operational capability with the 25 kiloton AN52 weapon was still awaited when EC 4 at Luxeuil sent its first pilots to train at Lahr in April 1966, prior to aircraft arriving at the HQ base from 14 October onwards, initially for EC 2/4 'La Fayette'. The wing's first squadron began flying IIIEs in February 1967, and a development of mild historical interest was the arrival of its first camouflaged aircraft on 23 August 1968. Previously all had worn natural metal finishes with national colours covering the whole rudder; gradually, this changed to dark green and dark grey disruptive upper surface camouflage with silver beneath, the IIIBs not starting to enter the scheme until 1980. Interceptor IIICs, however, went in for the blue-grey air superiority colour applied to Mirage F1s, though some reverted to the original markings by mid-1977. Resplendent in their tactical camouflage, EC 4's aircraft became the first in FATac to be declared operational with the AN52 and the wing will retain a nuclear role when re-equipped with Mirage 2000Ns (carrying ASMP stand-off weapons) in 1986-87.

Finally, Dijon-based EC 2 passed on its IIICs in order to gain the later model, the process

beginning on 5 April 1968 when EC 3/2 stood-down for conversion. Its aircraft started to arrive on 27 September — four days before EC 1/2 disposed of its IIICs. Having been the first with the IIIC and the last to take on IIIEs, EC 1/2 once again qualified as the premier French fighter squadron in 1984 when it received Mirage 2000Cs.

Production of AA Mirage IIIEs ended early in 1973 with what was officially the 183rd aircraft. In fact the numbering range extended from 401 up to 625 because of transfers to several foreign customers of aircraft originally laid down for local use.

A movement in the opposite direction concerned 50 Mirage 5Js constituting an embargoed Israeli order. After some deliberation and delay, compensation was agreed and the aircraft purchased for AA use after modification to French standards as Mirage 5Fs by the maintenance unit (Entrepôt de l'Armée de l'Air 601) at Chateaudun. The first to be completed, No 6, was delivered to Colmar on 5 April 1972 for new squadron EC 3/13 'Auvergne', formed on 1 May. Second and last to receive the windfall aircraft was another re-constituted unit, EC 3/3 'Ardennes', which was established at Nancy on 1 July 1974. Its eighth aircraft, received on 30 July, was the first camouflaged Mirage 5F. 'Ardennes' kept its new mounts only until February 1977, when they were supplanted by Jaguars and transferred to replace the IIIEs of EC 2/13.

Eight of the lowest-houred 5Fs were converted to Mirage 50FC standard to meet an urgent Chilean order of 1979, in return for which the AA was reportedly to have received eight brand-new 'pay-backs'. Two of these were delivered early in 1983, and a further pair was noted during the following year. By the spring of 1985, the AA was operating all of its eight replacements, these being amongst the last Mirage III/5/50s built.

It will be some years before the last Mirage III

leaves French service, and delays with funding shortages in the Mirage F1CR and 2000 programmes suggest that operational lives will have to be stretched as far as possible. Indeed, plans at one time called for Mirage IIIE withdrawals to begin in 1977 and be completed by 1985 whereas, in reality, not one had voluntarily gone to the scrap yard by 1984. In any case, disposal would hardly be seemly in view of the fact that final export versions of the first-generation Mirage were still coming off the production line as this book was being written! As the following chapter shows, Dassault has sophisticated or simplified the Mirage to meet customers' requirements, producing a plethora of variants with wide applications.

Of over 1,400 first-generation Mirages produced (excluding Israeli manufacture), two-thirds have been exported across the world from Abu Dhabi to Zaire. Individual requirements have, of course, differed, in response to which Dassault has modified the basic design to customers' preferences and varied the complexity of avionics to suit each need.

The earliest major change to the Mirage followed Australian interest and involved installation of a Rolls-Royce RB.146 Avon Mk 67, providing 12,000lb (5,670kg) of dry thrust and 16,000lb (7,260kg) with afterburning. No major surgery was involved in fitting the new engine, and with its greater power yet lower specific fuel comsumption than the Atar 09C, the Avon appeared the logical choice for all export Mirages. Having evaluated the Mirage IIIA prototype in June 1960, the Royal Australian Air Force undertook a similar exercise with the Avon Mirage IIIO No 1, named *City of Hobart*, following its initial flight on 13 February the next year, but in the end the Australians opted for the standard model as the performance of its rival was deemed insufficient to warrant its extra expense. There were also plans at this time to offer the

Avon-engined Mirage as a standard export model, fitted with Ferranti Airpass II fire-control radar (as in the English Electric Lightning), but this was abandoned when Australian interest ended.

Early customers were exclusively for the all-weather Mirage with its Cyrano radar nose, but it was clear that other potential purchasers did not want, or could not afford such sophistication. Thus the Mirage 5 (originally but briefly employing the Roman numeral V) was produced to meet an

Right:
Representative of today's Mirage IIIE, No 438 '13-QM' of EC 1/13 'Artois' poses before a hardened shelter during an exchange visit to Gilze-Rijen in the Netherlands during 1984. *Herman J. Sixma*

Below right:
With the blur of an Alouette III helicopter in the background to emphasize speed, a Mirage IIIE of EC 1/13 is caught at the moment of lift-off with full after-burner. *Herman J. Sixma*

Below:
Australia decided that it would not be worth the additional expense to have its Mirages powered by the Rolls-Royce Avon, and thus the prototype Mirage IIIO remained unique.

Israeli request for a simple ground-attack fighter which would retain rough field operability and carry more ordnance, yet be simpler to maintain and faster to turn round.

First flown on 19 May 1967, Mirage 5 No 01 featured the fuselage and engine of a Mirage IIIE, plus Mach 2 performance, whilst increasing weapon attachment points (including the centre-line) to seven and adding a further 500litre (110Imp gal) of internal fuel. To the external observer, the most obvious change was deletion of the large nose radome and re-positioning of the pitot tube to allow a ranging radar to be installed, if required. As such the Mirage 5 would carry up to 4,000kg (8,820lb) of stores in the ground-attack role or could perform as a day interceptor with two

AIM-9 Sidewinder AAMs and another 4,700litre (1,034Imp gal) of external fuel. According to Dassault claims, the aircraft required 15 hours of maintenance per flying hour, compared with 35:1 for a Lockheed Starfighter and 50:1 in the case of a McDonnell Phantom.

Above:
Various levels of avionics fitment are available to Mirage 50 customers, the upper end of the scale being represented by the addition of Cyrano IV or Agave radar.

Though many were satisfied with the revised configuration, others wanted a little more than the basic avionics — and some, a lot more. Ready and willing to oblige, Dassault produced a second broad range of tailor-made fighters optimised for interceptor, ground-attack or reconnaissance missions and identified by suffix letters combining

the role and customer, such that the designation 'Mirage 5' has become meaningless. As an example of the diversity, Abu Dhabi's Mirage 5EADs have the Cyrano radar and Doppler which makes them far closer to the French IIIE than the original Israeli 5J.

For the next major advance Dassault installed a

Overleaf – Left:
Belgium's sole tactical reconnaissance unit, No 42 Squadron, is equipped with Mirage 5BRs from a total of 27 originally purchased. Note the characteristic camera nose. *Herman J. Sixma*

Below:
Abu Dhabi, as principal member of the United Arab Emirates, has placed several Mirage orders, including one for three Mirage 5RAD reconnaissance models.

Right:
The Balzac V was France's first venture into VTOL, and, like the aircraft which followed, it relied on the wasteful principle of vertically-mounted lift engines.

more powerful version of the Atar, the 9K-50, to produce the appropriately-named Mirage 50. The modification was first effected during 1974 in new-build aircraft for South Africa, although these were known as Mirage IIIR2Z and IIID2Z models. What is regarded as the 'prototype' Mirage 50 (actually a conversion of the experimental Mirage Milan) was flown on 15 April 1975.

The Mirage 50 has now taken over from earlier models as the current variant on offer, even though recent follow-up batches from old customers have been of original types for reasons of commonality. Rated at 7,200kg (15,870lb) with reheat, the 9K-50 engine — which also powers the Mirage F1 — gives between 17 and 23% more thrust compared with the 09C. In terms of performance this means a 15-20% shorter take-off run, increased climb rate, better manoeuvrability, faster acceleration and a larger weapon or external fuel load.

Mirage 50s can combine the full range of stores, armament and equipment of Mirage III and 5 models with an inertial navigation system, head-up display and a radar or 'solid' nose. For multi-mode operation a Cyrano IVM radar bestows a capability equivalent to the Mirage IIIE (including interception with MATRA R.530 semi-active radar-homing AAMs), whereas Agave radar is fitted to attack-optimised aircraft, such as those armed with Aérospatiale AM-39 Exocet anti-ship missiles. Dassault has received at least one contract for installation of 9K-50 engines in earlier aircraft, this being a straightforward operation, the outside evidence of which is a curved leading edge

to take air intake splitter plate, rather than the original straight unit. It is possible that others will come forward to have their aircraft updated in the same way, doubtless with simultaneous fitment of an improved nav/attack system.

However, the Mirage 50 is still not the ultimate version of the mid-1950s delta to appear in Dassault's brochures. Taking part in the 1983 Paris Salon (following its first flight by Patrick Experton on the previous 21 December, having been converted from 50-01), the Mirage 3NG is now seeking customers, although none had come forward at the time of writing. Suffix letters indicating 'Nouvelle Génération' are appropriate for an aircraft incorporating the latest technology, and though it might seem unkind to dub the 3NG as a poor man's Mirage 2000, it has clearly been produced for countries unable to afford a top-of-the-line fighter.

Immediately apparent are the Kfir-like canards mounted on the engine air intakes, beneath which will be seen leading edge wing extensions (APEX). An in-flight refuelling probe may be fitted ahead of the cockpit (à la Mirage F1C-200), but many other improvements are concealed within. The 3NG has inherited features from the later Mirage 2000, of which the most significant is a full fly-by-wire control system. Replacing the old punched-card

Below:
In the markings of No 2 OCU at Williamtown is a Commonwealth CA.29 — better known as a Mirage IIIO(F). Camouflage has been added to Australian Mirages, but the colourful fin insignia have survived.

navigation unit is an inertial platform, backed by a CRT head-up display and optional sensors including Cyrano IV or Agave radar and a laser ranger. No less than nine strongpoints are available for stores, five of them beneath the fuselage, and three of these (centreline and wing inboard) are suitable for a four-bomb adaptor. Two DEFA 30mm cannon comprise the fixed internal armament.

In order to cover Mirage III, 5 and 50 exports in detail, it is convenient to review the operators in alphabetical sequence. It should be assumed that Mirage IIIs are radar equipped (apart from reconnaissance and trainer versions) and Mirage 5s are non-radar (except for a ranger in some cases) unless otherwise stated.

Abu Dhabi   As the major component of the United Arab Emirates Air Force, the ADAF placed its first Mirage order in September 1972 and took delivery of a dozen Mirage 5AD attack aircraft and two 5DAD trainers in 1974, operating them from the local airport. Due to a shortage of trained pilots, the aircraft were flown by Pakistanis

Top:
Serving in Brazilian markings, the Mirage IIIEBR has the local designation F-103E.

Above:
A non-standard blue and grey camouflage scheme is worn by Chilean Mirages — in this case by the second of two Mirage 50DC trainers.

Overleaf:
A JATO by the prototype Mirage IVP conversion shows clearly the pylon-mounted Aérospatiale ASMP nuclear missile which distinguishes this variant. Two squadrons will operate most of the 18 Mirage IVs being modified to this standard.

Above right:
Typical air defence armament of the Mirage F1 in French service — modelled by an F1B — is a pair of underwing MATRA Super 530s, plus MATRA 550 Magics on the wingtips. Training versions of the latter, lacking forward fins, are fitted to this aircraft.

Below right:
Twenty Mirage F1B two-seat trainers have been delivered to the Armée de l'Air for pilot conversion. Almost all are operated from Orange by ET 3/5 'Combat Venaissin'.

Above:
Colombia's Grupo Aéreo de Combate 1 received 14
Mirage 5COAs for ground attack from July 1971
onwards. These were to have been updated with Israeli
avionics in the early 1980s, but financial problems
intervened.

Below:
Saudi Arabia funded Egypt's first batch of Mirages,
including this 5SDD trainer, and the Saudi national
markings were thus applied for delivery.

Above:
Orange fin and wingtips are evident on this Egyptian Mirage 5SDR recce aircraft, pictured in 1983.

under an agreement allowing them to be leased to Pakistan in an emergency. Further Mirages followed in 1976-77, comprising three 5RAD tactical reconnaisance models, a third 5DAD and 14 multi-role 5EADs, the latter (as previously noted) being virtually Mirage IIIEs, with Cyrano radar and Doppler. Their armament includes MATRA Magic AAMs. Mirages now operate from a military base at Maquatra/al Dhafra: 5EADs and 5DADs in I Shaheen Squadron, and 5ADs and 5RADs in II Shaheen Squadron. They are being augmented by Mirage 2000s.

Argentina   Following evaluation against the BAC Lightning and Northrop F-5A an order for 10 Mirage IIIEAs and two IIIDA trainers was placed in October 1970 for air defence duties with the Comando Aéreo de Defensa of Argentina's Air Force, the Fuerza Aérea Argentina (FAA). Deliveries inside FAA Lockeed Hercules began in September 1972, the first aircraft flying in South America during July 1973. Armed with MATRA R.530s, the Mirages are stationed at BAM Mariano Moreno, which in 1979 was promoted to Group status as the VIII Brigada Aérea, on arrival of a further seven IIIEAs from a 1977 order. Operated by 1er Escuadron de Caza-Interceptora, which is the sole squadron of Grupo 8 de Caza, they were issued with MATRA 550 Magic infra-red AAMs shortly before the Falklands war of April-June 1982. No replacements have been ordered from Dassault for the two shot down

during the conflict, but soon afterwards, in December 1982, the FAA received a pair of second-hand IIIBE trainers from French surplus.

An urgent requirement for attack aircraft during mid-1978, when Argentina was on the brink of war with Chile, resulted in an order for 36 IAI Daggers and three trainers. Equivalent to Mirage 5s, the daggers were obtained for $185million after refurbishment in Israel, and were assigned to Grupo 6 de Caza-Bombardeo of the VI Brigada Aérea at Tandil. As the result of losses during the

Overleaf – Left:
The formal entry into service of the Mirage 2000C was marked by a mass 'taxi-in' of a dozen aircraft at Dijon on 2 July 1984.

Above right:
EC 1/2 'Cigognes' — the famed 'Stork' squadron of the French Air Force — was first to receive Mirage IIICs, in July 1961. Exactly 23 years later it commissioned as the premier Mirage 2000C unit.

Below right:
The attractive lines of the Mirage 2000C are becoming an increasingly common sight in French skies with the continuing re-equipment of EC 2. This pair serve with the first squadron to equip, EC 1/2 'Cigognes'.
Andre van Haute

Falklands war (described later) an emergency delivery of 10 Mirage 5Ps was made by Peru on 6 June 1982, but hostilities ended before they could be put into action. They were allocated the serials of destroyed Daggers and can be identified as later additions only by careful study of aerial shapes and positions.

A further, quite remarkable, cargo arrived at Buenos Aires by sea on 18 December 1982 in the form of the first aircraft in a batch of 19 Mirage IIICJ interceptors and three IIIBJ trainers, also from Israeli surplus. These, the survivors of two Middle East wars, are based at El Plumerillo (IV Brigada Aérea) with Grupo 4 de Caza.

Australia After the evaluation (described above) to find a replacement for the Common-wealth (North American) Avon Sabre, an initial contract for 30 Mirage IIIOs was placed in October 1960, increasing first to 62 and then 100. In parallel, 10 IIID trainers were ordered, followed by a further six in October 1970. The first two Mirages were produced by Dassault, formal hand-over of the first taking place at Melun-Villa-roche on 9 April 1963, but the others were assembled at Avalon, Victoria, by the Common-wealth of Australia Government Aircraft Factor-ies, which bestowed the local type number CA.29.

Commonwealth assembled the next two Mirages from major components supplied by Dassault, and the first of these flew on 16 November 1963 and was taken on charge on 20 December that year (officially the date was 29 January 1964, when the Minister for Air, Mr Fairhall, accepted the logbooks of the first new aircraft). The next six had French fuselages and wings but Australian equipment, and a further five featured a small number of critical components from Dassault. Thereafter production was from local resources, the last single-seat aircraft going to the Royal Australian Air Force (RAAF) in December 1968. GAF's first trainer flew on 6 October 1966 and was delivered on 10 November the same year. Fuse-lages for all the two-seat aircraft came from France, local production halting temporarily with the 10th aircraft in July 1967. A follow-up contract for six more trainers was placed in October 1970 and completed in 1972.

Single-seat Mirages came in two varieties: IIIO(F) interceptor with Cyrano IIA radar and MATRA R.530 AAMs — these were the first 50 RAAF aircraft — and IIIO(A) featuring Cyrano IIB, Doppler nav/attack equipment and radio altimeter, for ground attack. The IIIO(F) was a

short-lived variant, for all survivors were converted to IIIO(A) standard between October 1968 and February 1971, later replacing their natural metal finish by camouflage. No 2 OCU at Williamtown equipped with Mirages early in 1964, also receiving trainer versions, and No 75 Squadron received its first IIIO(F)s in July 1965, becoming operational on 2 August 1965, prior to taking up station at Butterworth, Malaysia, in May 1967. No 76 Squadron re-equipped with interceptors from September 1966 for local service and then disbandment, whilst in February 1967 No 3 arrived at Williamtown from Butterworth to receive IIIO(A) models, which it took back to Malaysia in February 1969. Finally, No 77 moved to Williamtown in July 1969, also to take on IIIO(A)s.

Delays with selection of a successor resulted in a life-extension programme for RAAF aircraft, beginning in 1979 and including replacement of fatigued mainplanes, modifications to engine and avionics, the addition of laser-guided bombs, and purchase (in 1981) of MATRA Magics to replace the limited-capability AIM-9B Sidewinder AAMs. At last, in October 1981, the McDonnell Douglas F/A-18 Hornet was chosen as a follow-on, and first steps towards re-equipment were taken on 10 August 1983 when No 75 Squadron moved to Williamtown from Butterworth, to be followed in 1987 by No 3. First Hornet recipient will be No 2 OCU in 1985, followed by No 75 Squadron in June 1986, No 3 in July 1987 and No 77 in April 1988.

Belgium On 16 February 1968 the Belgian Government announced its decision to replace Republic F-84F Thunderstreaks and RF-84F Thunderflashes with 54 Mirage 5BA attack aircraft, 22 5BR tactical reconnaissance models and 12 5BD trainers, with options (all eventually taken up) of nine, five and four respectively. Apart from the first one of each model, assembly was by the local firm SABCA in collaboration with Avions Fairey and other, smaller contractors.

With US avionics, and generally more sophisticated in terms of systems than the 'bare' Mirage 5, the first 5BA flew at Bordeaux on 6 March 1970, closely followed by the initial trainer on the 31st of the month, the 5BR joining it in the air on 16 October 1970. The two-seater was taken on

Left:
Carrying an Aérospatiale ASMP nuclear stand-off weapon on the centreline and a pair of self-defence Magic AAMs, the prototype Mirage 2000N reveals the operational configuration of France's latest strike aircraft.

Below left:
A twin-engined delta suited for long-range interdiction and air superiority roles, the Mirage 4000 has been unable to secure an order from home or abroad despite rumours of Saudi Arabian interest.

charge by the Force Aérienne Belge/Belgische Luchtmacht on 27 April 1970, while the first locally-assembled examples to be accepted were attack aircraft BA02 on 8 August and trainer BD02 three days later. At Florennes, 8 Escadrille/Smaldeel of 2 Wing re-formed on 15 July 1970 with eight French-trained pilots and began student training on 5 October, soon attaining its authorised strength of 12 BDs and six BAs. The unit moved to 3 Wing at Bierset on 15 December 1971.

No 2 Esc/Smd converted to Mirage 5BAs during 1971 within 2 Wing, but No 1 Esc/Smd received its 5BAs in 3 Wing from January 1972 onwards. The recce aircraft are operated by 42 Esc/Smd, which

received its first at Bierset in July 1971 before moving to 2 Wing at Florennes on 15 September 1971. Local Mirage production ended early in 1973, the final delivery (BA63) taking place on 13 July. No retirement date has been set for the aircraft, but it is known that 2 Wing will convert to General Dynamics F-16 Fighting Falcons from 1987, after which all will be concentrated in 3 Wing until the end of their useful lives.

Brazil Mirages constitute the prime inteceptor element of the Forca Aérea Brasileira following the placing of an order for 12 Mirage IIIEBRs and four IIIDBR trainers on 12 May 1970, these receiving the local type designations F-103E and F-103D respectively. The first aircraft was handed over in France on 31 May 1972 and training of personnel undertaken at Dijon, Mont-de-Marsan and Cazaux between June and October that year. A follow-on order in 1978

Below:
Pakistan placed its first Mirage order in 1967 for 18 IIIEP all-weather interceptors armed with R.530 and Magic AAMs. These serve at Sargodha with No 5 Squadron.

Above:
The Peruvian combat force includes the Mirage 5DP two-seat trainer variant.

Anapolis, near Brasilia. Licensed production of Mirage IIIs and purchase of 50 Mirage 50s has been mooted in the past, but without result.

covered four F-103Es, whilst the loss of three trainers in 1980-82 resulted in two Mirage IIIBEs being delivered in 1984. Mirages are operated by 1 and 2 Esquadroes of 1 Grupo de Difesa Aérea (known as 1 Ala de DA until 11 April 1979) at

Chile   The tension between Chile and Argentina which resulted in the latter obtaining IAI Daggers also saw the Fuerza Aérea de Chile place an urgent order for 16 Mirage 50s in July 1979. Apart from South African IIIR2Zs and IIID2Zs,

this was the first contract for the 9K-50 engined variant as such, an earlier requirement from Sudan for 14 50SOs and two 50SOD trainers having fallen through. Eight low-houred Armée de l'Air Mirage 5Fs were converted by Dassault into Mirage 50FCs, whilst Chilean pilots trained at Dijon and ground crew received instruction at the École Technique, Rochefort. Deliveries by sea began in June 1980, the first aircraft flying again at Antofagasta two months later, in time for re-formation of Grupo 4 on 15 September 1980, this now being a component of II Brigada Aérea. Early in 1984 reports that Chile had ordered a further three Mirage 50s were denied in Paris, but approval was given for transfer of a second-hand Mirage IIIB trainer from French stocks.

Mirages were initially based at Arturo Merino Benitez Airport, and then moved to Iquique, although they will ultimately take up residence at the new base of Santo Domingo de las Rocas. Eight new Mirage 50Fs (radar-equipped) joined the unit in 1982-83, together with two 50DC trainers. Their main duty is ground attack.

Colombia   Replacement of Canadair Sabres in Grupo Aéreo de Combate 1 of the Fuerza Aérea Colombiana was effected through a 1970 order for 14 Mirage 5COA ground-attack aircraft, two reconnaissance 5CORs and a pair of 5COD

trainers, first deliveries of which were made in September 1971, July 1973 and November 1971 respectively, to German Olano air base. During the mid-1980s the Grupo established detachments at Barranquitta and San Andres. Late in 1981 a contract was placed with IAI for 12 Kfir C2s (the first export order for this aircraft), these intended to replace Lockheed T-33As of Grupo Aéreo de Combate 2, also at German Olano. At the same time, plans were made for Israeli technicians to update the avionics of the remaining 16 Mirage 5s to Kfir-type standards during 1983. Severe financial problems intervened, and both the Kfir purchase and the update were cancelled before they could be implemented.

Ecuador   Having been thwarted in its attempts to obtain 24 IAI Kfirs by a US embargo on sales of the J79 engine in Latin America, the Fuerza Aérea Ecuatoriana ordered Mirage F1s in 1977. It later considered the Atar-engined IAI Nesher without much interest. Changed US policies resulted in a relaxation of the J79 ban in 1979 and three years later a contract was signed for 12 Kfir C2s and an option on a similar number.

Egypt   The first Egyptian order for Mirages was placed in September 1973 and funded by Saudi Arabia, with the result that the 32 5SDE Cyrano-equipped interceptors and six 5SDD trainers (the first three of each diverted from French contracts) were delivered in Saudi markings after training of pilots in France. Direct orders followed from Cairo, comprising 14 non-radar 5SSEs in December 1975, eight 5SSEs and six tactical recce 5SDRs in November 1977, and 16 Mirage 5E2s in June 1980. The last-mentioned, delivered in 1983-84, feature an updated nav/attack system based on the Alpha Jet NGEA and including a SAGEM ULISS 81 inertial platform and Thomson-CSF TMV 630 laser range-finder. Mirages are based at Tanta (including an OCU) and Genaclis (including the 5SDRs), eight of them forming the national aerobatic team. Egypt has also ordered Mirage 2000s.

Gabon   The initial order by Gabon for modern combat aircraft was placed in mid-1975 and called for three Mirage 5G attack types, two 5RG recce aircraft and two 5DG trainers to be based at Libreville. Deliveries took place in 1978, although the 5RGs were cancelled. Agreement to supply a further six aircraft was reached following a visit to

Left:
Having previously bought Mirage IIICZs, South Africa followed on with 17 IIIEZ variants for both interceptor and attack missions.

51

Gabon by President Mitterrand in January 1983, these being reported as four Mirage 5Gs and two 5DG trainers. The first of each type appeared early in 1984, the single-seat aircraft being designated Mirage 5G-II, and according to unconfirmed reports these are Libyan aircraft confiscated whilst being overhauled in France. More than six extra aircraft may now be in prospect, possibly including redundant French IIICs and IIIBs.

Israel A simplified version of the Mirage IIIC (lacking, among other features, provision for an SEPR rocket pack) was ordered in 1960. La Tsvah Hagana Le Israel/Heyl Ha'Avir took delivery of 72 IIICJs between 4 July 1961 and 22 July 1964, in company with five IIIBJ trainers between 16 February 1966 and 12 January 1968. These were involved in air combats with Arab forces and at least two later acquired camera noses. The survivors — 19 IIICJs and three IIIBJs — were sold to Argentina in 1982.

Israel was the first Mirage 5 customer, with a contract for 50 plus two 5DJ trainers in 1966. The first single-seat 5J was flown on 19 May 1967, just over a fortnight before the Six Day War resulted in a French embargo on all new military exports to Israel. The two trainers were cancelled and the 50 5Js, completed between 12 September 1967 and

Below:

Below:
The unique Swiss Mirage IIICS was acquired in December 1962 for trials work, although it carried the legend 'Mirage IIIC' on the nose.

19 June 1969, were placed in storage at EAA 601, Chateaudun. They were eventually bought by the French Government as Mirage 5Fs. Israel produced an unlicensed copy of the Mirage 5 which led to the Kfir.

Lebanon   A 1965 order for 12 aircraft and 15 MATRA R.530 AAMs included 10 Mirage IIIELs, the prototype of which first flew on 25 July 1967. Deliveries were effected between 11 September 1967 and 11 March 1969, accompanied by two IIIBL trainers (on 14 June 1968 and 11 March 1969), although four interceptors and a trainer were immediately placed in storage. The others have seen little use, and all have been periodically offered for sale or exchange, without success.

Libya   In November 1969, two months after a revolution had overthrown the monarchy, Libya placed a major contract for 110 Mirage 5s. Strange to relate, however, the first of the type to be seen in the country were five IIIBs from the French ECT 2/2 (Nos 204, 208, 211, 213 and 220) which wore Libyan insignia between 28 August and 4 September 1970. Carrying Libyan student pilots

and French instructors in a flypast over Tripoli to mark the first anniversary of the revolution, they stood in for aircraft still to be built for Al Quwwat al Jawwiya al Libiyya. It was 22 December 1970 before the first of 15 Mirage 5DD trainers was delivered to Dijon for instructional use, followed by the first of 32 5DE attack aircraft (equivalents of the IIIE, with Cyrano and Doppler) on 3 March 1971. The others went directly to Libya and comprised 53 5Ds with simplified avionics and 10 5DR recce aircraft, delivery beginning 5 November 1971 and March 1972 respectively. During the early 1980s many of these returned to Dassault's Toulouse plant for overhaul and it appears that five 5Ds and a 5DR were confiscated (and may have been presented to Gabon) by the French Government late in 1983 following Libyan intervention in the Chad civil war. Mirage 5s are based at Gemal Abdel Nasser (formerly the RAF station at El Adem) alongside Mirage F1s.

Pakistan   Four separate contracts have been placed by the Pakistan Fiza'ya for Mirages, the first in 1967 covering 18 IIIEP all-weather interceptors with MATRA R.530 and Magic AAMs delivered between 25 October 1967 and 30 April 1969, three IIIRPs between 10 April and 23 June 1969, and three IIIDP trainers, beginning 30 January 1969. A 1970 order involved 28 simplified Mirage 5PAs and two more IIIDPs, and in 1975 the recce element was strengthened by a contract for 10 additional IIIRPs. Finally, in 1979, Pakistan commissioned two 5DPA2 trainers, which were delivered from 20 September 1981

With flat land at a premium, valley-floor airfields are a common feature in Switzerland — as is a Mirage IIIS landing close to a village.

onwards, and 30 5PAs. The last 30 single-seat aircraft were more advanced Mirage 5s, comprising air-to-air 5PA2s with 26nm-range Cyrano IV radar and 5PA3s with 13nm-range Agave radar for surface roles, including carriage of AM-39 Exocet anti-ship missiles. Deliveries were completed on 29 December 1982.

No 5 Squadron at Sargodha received Mirage IIIEPs, while the Combat Commander's School at the same base also has a few 5PAs. At Rafiqui, No 9 OCU operates IIIDPs and 5PAs, and No 20 Squadron has IIIRPs, plus some 5PAs. The final 30 aircraft have gone to two units: No 8 Squadron at Masroor (5PA3) and No 33 at Shorkot Road (5PA2). A new Mirage rebuild factory at Kamra completed its first airframe and engine overhaul in February 1981, the stipulated lives being 11 years or 1,000 hours for the Mirage and 600 hours for its Atar. All the early Mirage IIIs have been fitted with improved avionics, including a Litton LW-33 nav/attack system.

Peru Mirage deliveries to the Fuerza Aérea Peruana initially involved 14 5P ground-attack aircraft between 7 May 1968 and 21 December 1969, plus two 5DP trainers on 30 September and 17 October 1968. Operated by Grupo 13 at Chiclayo, they were augmented by eight more 5Ps in 1974 and a single 5DP in March 1976, although 10 were transferred to Argentina in July 1982. Later orders reportedly increased procurement to 32 Mirage 5Ps and five trainers by 1981, and a fourth contract was announced in 1982 involving 5P3s with Cyrano IV radar, 5P4s with air-to-surface optimised Agave radar, and 5DP1 and 5DP3 trainers. These are almost certainly to be produced under a conversion contract signed in March 1983, through which Dassault is providing kits for systems modernisation of existing Mirages with Litton inertial platforms, Thomson-CSF head-up displays and a CSF laser range-finder. They will be reinforced by Mirage 2000s.

South Africa After an evaluation at Marignane in May 1961, Mirage III orders from the SAAF, or Suid Arfikaanse Lugmag, eventually totalled 58, begining with 16 IIICZ interceptors handed over between 18 December 1962 and 9 March 1964 to an April 1962 contract. The balance comprised three IIIBZ trainers (14 December 1962 to 9 December 1964), four IIIRZs for tactical recce (24 November 1966 to 22 February 1967), 17 interceptor/attack IIIEZs

(2 February 1965 to 15 March 1972), three IIIDZ trainers (4 July to 18 September 1969), 11 IIID2Z trainers and four IIIR2Zs. Those incorporating a 2 in their designations are powered by the Atar 9K-50 engine and in this respect are equivalent to the Mirage 50.

No 2 Squadron at Waterkloof accepted its first IIICZ in April 1963, adding IIIEZs in July 1965 — the latter remaining only until August 1966, when they joined a re-formed No 3 Squadron. No 85 Advanced Flying School (now known as No 85 Air Combat School) at Pietersburg received the IIID2Zs from October 1974 and soon afterwards took on the IIIEZs and IIIDZs from No 3 Squadron when that unit converted to Mirage F1s in April 1975. All other Mirage III variants are operated by No 2 Squadron, which is now at

Hoedspruit and has been involved in operations against neighbouring countries.

Early in 1985, plans were revealed for the SAAF's Mirage IIICZs to be refurbished with a new radar and fire control, plus canard foreplanes similar to those of the Kfir C2 — probably by Atlas Aircraft Corporation in collaboration with Israeli firms. If this programme goes ahead, some of the modified aircraft will form an extra Mirage unit within the Active Citizen Force (reserve). This will by No 5 Squadron, currently flying Atlas Impalas at Durban.

Spain Although Mirage IIIC No 42 was flown to Spain for evaluation on 3 April 1962, it was not until 1968 that an order was placed by the Ejército del Aire Español for 24 Mirage IIIEE interceptors and six IIIDE trainers, to be known under the local designations of C.11 and CE.11 respectively. Pilots began training at Dijon in March 1970 and transferred in the following month to Luxeuil, where the first IIIEE was accepted on 9 April. Rapid deliveries were made possible by transfers from production intended for France, with the result that the first six were flown from Dijon to Manises/Valencia on 13 June 1970, there to join

Below:
From opposite ends of South America, but brought together in a pre-delivery test flight over France, are a Mirage IIIEA of the Argentine Air Force (top) and a Venezuelan Mirage 5DV.

Escuadrones 101 and 102 of Ala de Caza 10, armed with MATRA R.530 and AIM-9 Sidewinder AAMs. The wing was re-designated in 1972 as Ala de Caza 11, comprising the 111 and 112 Escuadrones. Mirage IIIs have been complemented in air defence and secondary ground-attack roles by Mirage F1s and will by replaced by McDonnell Douglas Hornets in the mid-1980s.

Switzerland   After a comprehensive evaluation of contenders, including rough-field trials of IIIA No 6 and IIIC No 1 at Unterbach in January 1960, the Kommando der Flieger und Fliegerabwehrtruppen placed a contract in June 1961 for 100 Mirage IIIs to be built by Fabrique Federale d'Avions under a licence agreement, with Sulzer AG similarly providing the Atar engine. Local manufacture increased prices, however (the programme cost rocketed from SwFr830million to SwFr1,447million in just one year!), resulting in contracts being trimmed to 57 aircraft by 1964 — although four more trainers were added later.

Apart from a solitary Mirage IIICS used for trials from December 1962 onwards, Swiss aircraft were based on the IIIE. The resultant IIIS has the Hughes TARAN 18 (Tactical Attack Radar And Navigation) system for compatibility with Hughes HM-55 (AIM-26B) Falcon AAMs; provision for AIM-9 Sidewinder AAMs and Aérospatiale AS-30 ASMs; plus a strengthened fuselage, wing and undercarriage. Dassault provided two IIIs aircraft on 28 February and 1 June 1964 (the first having flown on 13 December 1963), and a further 34 came from FFA between 27 October 1965 and 7 February 1969, these going to Fliegerstaffeln 16 and 17 at Payerne which were commissioned with their first 24 aircraft on 2 March 1968. Dassault's second IIIS had flown on 8 January 1964 and spent the period July 1964 to August 1966 at Holloman AFB, USA, on nav/attack system trials.

A prototype of the recce Mirage IIIRS, with TARAN 1S and a camera nose, flew in France on 5 November 1964 and remained there until delivered on 27 July 1967. FFA supplied 17 more to Fliegerstaffel 10 at Dubendorf between 28 March 1968 and 12 June 1969. A pair of French-built IIIBS trainers were included in the initial contract. The first of these flew on 21 October 1963 and was delivered on 30 November. Two IIIBS trainers were added in 1970-72 (the second of which was locally assembled from French parts), whilst the most recent arrivals from Dassault — on 27 January and 3 February 1983 — have been two IIIDS operational trainers. The current squadron dispositions are FlgStff 10 with flights of IIIRS aircraft at Payerne, Sion and Stans (Buochs); FlfStff 16 at Stans (Buochs); and FlgStff 17 at Payerne.

Switzerland is planning a life-extension programme for all remaining Mirages involving the addition of canards on the air intakes and strakes on the radome to improve handling and stability at high angles of attack. The installations were tested on a Mirage IIIRS in 1984 and will be accompanied by strengthening of mainplanes.

Venezuela   Deliveries of an order by the Fuerzas Aéreas Venezolanas for 15 Mirages began with the first of four Mirage 5Vs in November 1972, these quickly being followed by nine IIIEV interceptors from May 1973 and two 5DV trainers beginning February 1973. An attrition-replacement IIIEV was added in 1977, and all remaining aircraft now serve with Escuadrón 36 of Grupo de Caza 12 at Barquisimeto.

Zaire   Mirage procurement by the Force Aerienne Zaîroise was curtailed as the result of financial problems, and a 1975 requirement for three squadrons was reduced to just 14 Mirage 5Ms and three 5DM trainers, not all of which may have been received when deliveries were effected in 1975. The aircraft are operated by 211e Escadrille of the 21e Wing de Chasse et d'Assaut at Kamina.

Below:
The sole Mirage squadron in Zaire is the 211ᵉ Escadrille, based at Kamina. Its equipment includes three Mirage IIIDM trainers.

Few aircraft of the present era have been involved in combats as diverse as those witnesed by the Mirage III and 5 — although it was inevitable that with Israel as an early purchaser the aircraft would soon become involved in the regular Middle East conflicts. Parkistan's battles with India provided another arena for it to show its mettle, whilst out of the limelight, Mirages have been involved in South Africa's operations against its neighbours. Most recently, the skies over the Falkland Islands have seen Argentine Mirages and Daggers suffering heavy losses to Sea Harriers and surfaced-based weapons.

It began on 20 August 1963 when two Mirage IIICJs of the Israel Defence Force/Air Force were scrambled to intercept eight Syrian MiG-17s which had penetrated the border at 20,000ft. Gaining an extra 6,500ft on their quarry, the Mirages dived on to the unwitting formation and hacked down two MiGs with their 30mm cannon before the others knew what was happening. In a few seconds the IDF/AF had given a convincing demonstration of its new combat aircraft and instilled caution into potential opponents. Those who hoped that the more advanced MiG-21 would prove a match for the Mirage were to be disappointed on 14 November 1964 when one of four was lost in an air battle with two IIICJs.

Below:
This pre-delivery line-up, which could at first sight be of IIICs for France, is revealed as comprising aircraft destined for Israel by close examination of data printed on the rudder. The first four aircraft are Mirage IIICJs Nos 35, 33, 32 and 34.

Above:
Israel was an early customer for the Mirage and gained numerous air combat successes with the aircraft. A Mirage IIICJ here escorts an El Al Boeing 707.

These and subsequent skirmishes were but a rehearsal for the conflict to come, when on 5 June 1967 the IDF/AF launched a crushing pre-emptive strike against its enemies at the start of the Six Day War. In the vanguard were three formations, each of 40 aircraft — Mirage IIIs and Super Mystères (another Dassault product) — which devastated Egypt's major airfields and destroyed or damaged 300 aircraft on the ground during three hours of high-intensity attacks. Such was the tempo that Egypt believed the US or Britain to be aiding the Israelis, but the pressure was maintained by rapid turn-rounds at home bases.

Ground crew worked frantically to replace fuel, ammunition and oxygen in seven minutes, rather than the usual 20, allowing Mirages to fly 12 sorties per day each. Thus, after Egypt had been dealt with, the Israelis were able to inflict similar damage on Jordan and Syria later the same day. Air-to-air combats were restricted to a few successful fights with Egyptian MiG-19s and MiG-21s. Mirages featured prominently in the war

as interceptors and attack aircraft, and only a small number are believed to have been lost.

It was a different story in the early days of the Yom Kippur war, when Egyptian and Syrian forces were the ones to achieve surprise with their attack on 6 October 1973. By this time, Israel was producing its own Mirage 5s as the Nesher, these joining the IIICJs in combat for the first time. In addition, from 14 October onwards, Libyan Mirages were seen over the battle zone, reportedly contributing 400 sorties from Egyptian bases.

Rapid delivery of US supplies, including 'smart' weapons and electronic countermeasures to the SAMs which initially took a heavy toll of IDF/AF aircraft, allowed Israel to avert a disastrous situation, though its losses up to the cease-fire of 24 October included 12 Mirages. Four of these were claimed by the Egyptian MiG-21 pilot Ali Wagedy, to add to two of the same type obtained in 1970. Israel is reluctant to name its successful pilots, yet it is safe to say that the IDF/AF holds the world's top-scoring jet ace — probably with several of these victories obtained with the Mirage.

Spectacular air-to-air victories (85 to nil) were claimed against Syria between 7 and 28 June 1982, by which time F-15 Eagles and F-16 Fighting Falcons were the main IDF/AF interceptors. In this instance, combat was over Lebanon, and IAI

Kfirs (making their large-scale debut in battle) and F-4 Phantoms were credited with undertaking the majority of precision strikes against ground targets — including 19 SAM sites.

More modest scores were attained by Pakistan's Mirage IIIEPs in the December 1971 war with India which led to the birth of Bangladesh. Air combat and ground attack were the two roles in which the Mirage was employed, claims being made for 10 Indian aircraft, eight of them in the air: five Hunters (four on 5 December), two Su-7s and a Canberra. The IAF alleged destruction of six Mirages, yet after the war Pakistan was able to show the world's press 23 of the 24 received up to that time, the other having been lost in an accident.

Much less is known of South Africa's Mirage III operations and claims that some of its aircraft were based in Rhodesia (now Zimbabwe) during the guerilla war of the 1970s. Certainly, however, Mirage IIIs and F1s have been used in extensive ground-attack operations against regular and irregular forces in Mosambique and Angola, the latter having lost MiG-21s to SAAF Mirages of unknown type on 6 November 1981 and 5 October 1982. According to camera-gun film, a Mirage F1CZ was responsible for at least one of the MiG kills.

Faulty tactics and geography appear to have frustrated the Mirage during the Falklands war of 1982, Argentina's IIIEA interceptors starting (and virtually ending) their participation with a disastrous combat on 1 May. After an early inconclusive action on that first day of Britain's fight to regain the disputed islands, Sea Harriers shot down one Mirage and crippled another (which was finished off by 'friendly' AA whilst making an emergency landing). This came as a severe shock to the planners who had rated the Sea Harrier easy meat and resulted in the remainder of the force being husbanded for all-weather defence of the mainland — in which role they were never to be called to action.

Both Mirage and Harrier were operating at the limit of their combat radius when they met. The Mirages preferred to occupy the 'high ground' where their supersonic speed was of advantage, whilst the Sea Harriers were happy to remain at lower levels and derive benefit from excellent

Below:
A Mirage IIIBJ trainer of the Israel Defence Force. The squadron insignia on the fin has been blacked out by the censor.

manoeuvrability. First attempts by Mirage IIIs to dive on a Harrier combat air patrol saw their missiles pass well clear of target, and when they tried to mix it on the Harriers' terms, losses were rapidly sustained.

Following the decision to keep Argentina's sole all-weather interceptors outside the war zone, the fighter-bombers (Douglas Skyhawks and IAI Daggers) were obliged to raid British forces at low level without escort. This complicated the defence, but when the attackers were caught in the open they suffered grievously. Perhaps prematurely, Argentina had conceded air superiority to Britain within hours of the 'real' shooting starting — and if any in Buenos Aires thought victory was possible without this fundamental prerequisite of modern warfare they were soon to be disillusioned.

Daggers — Israeli-built versions of the Mirage 5 — were equally hard-pressed as fighter-bombers, losing 11 of their number in the combat zone (nine to Sea Harriers and two to SAMs) plus six more which almost made home but crashed or were found to be damaged beyond repair. The latter category may include some which used their fuel-thirsty afterburners for too long whilst trying to evade interception over the islands and were

forced to ditch on the way back. If this latest combat shows the Mirage in a less than favourable light, it should be remembered that the aircraft's earlier successes were in the hands of air arms which had already gained the ascendency (moral or actual) over their opponents. This was not the case in 1982, yet taking the aircraft's combat record as a whole, it may be said with some certainty (lack of precise Israeli data making an exact statement impossible) that the Mirage has achieved an air-to-air record well in excess of 1 : 1.

Above:
Argentina's Mirage IIIEAs played little part in the Falklands war after a disastrous first day of operations. They were held back to defend the mainland against air attacks which never materialised.

Below:
The Israeli-built Dagger suffered heavy casualties in Argentine service whilst running the gauntlet of Sea Harrier patrols during bombing raids on the British Fleet. The defences shot down 11, but another six were abandoned on the way home or damaged beyond repair when landing.

Some experimental models of the original Mirage family formed the basis of production versions and have been described in the foregoing text; others were destined to remain one-offs and so are included in this catch-all chapter for completeness. Also to be described below in brief terms are Israel's Mirage 5 copies and developments — these being part of the mirage story despite their different designations.

First, though, it is convenient to dispose of here those Mirage IIIs which failed even to achieve the transition into metal. Included in these are the IIIK offered to Britain with a Rolls-Royce Spey afterburning turbofan; IIIM navalised version schemed for France's Marine Nationale; and the IIIW lightweight fighter which would have been built by Boeing as a parallel to the Northrop F-5. One engine development aircraft may also be dealt with at this juncture, namely the IIIC2. Powered by an Atar 09K-6 optimised for high-altitude interception, this was a conversion of IIIE No 406 and first flew on 10 May 1965, being lost in an accident at Solenzara, Corsica, on 3 October 1968 after return to its original standard.

One of the earliest — and certainly the most radical — modifications to the Mirage III was to bestow vertical take-off capability. The impetus was provided by a NATO specification (NBMR 3) which requested a VTOL combat aircraft able to operate independently of vulnerable airfields, and

it provoked great activity in the drawing offices of manufacturers throughout Europe and the US. Britain already had the revolutionary vectored-thrust Hawker P.1127 flying and was working on the definitive P.1154, but France chose to adopt the less efficient system of vertical lift engines in its contender.

Appropriately designated Mirage IIIV, this was to be preceded by two trials aircraft: one to gain VTOL experience, and the other to flight-test the intended forward thrust engine. The first of these was none other than the Mirage III prototype, No 001, which underwent a 15-month modification by Sud Aviation and emerged with four pairs of Rolls-Royce RB.108 Stage 1a lift engines fed from inconspicuous intakes above the centre fuselage and a Bristol Siddeley Orpheus B.Or 3 replacing the Atar for forward flight. Each of the eight RB.108s weighed 274lb (124kg) and developed 2,210lb (1,002kg) of thrust for take-off (with 11% air bleed for stabilising jets), whilst the Orpheus was rated at 5,000lb (2,268kg) thrust. All-up weight of the aircraft was 14,330lb (6,500kg).

Below:
The unique Mirage IIIC2 No 01 was converted from a Mirage IIIE and fitted with an Atar 09K-6 engine for improved high-altitude performance. Note that Doppler is deleted.

Marked on its fin as the 'Dassault Sud Balzac V 001' (the nickname deriving from the coincidence of its designation corresponding with the telephone number of a well-known Paris advertising agency) the half-thrust, half-weight test model for the IIIV made its first tethered hop at Melun-Villaroche on 12 October 1962 with Rene Bigand in command. A conventional flight followed on 1 March and the first transition on 18 March (the Balzac's 17th sortie). Flight No 19, on 29 March, saw the first complete cycle — vertical take-off, conventional flight and vertical landing — four months ahead of schedule.

Further useful data was gathered by the Balzac until, on its 125th flight, on 27 January 1964, it crashed during roll testing, killing Jacques Pinier of the CEV. It was possible to salvage the airframe, and so V 001 returned to flying until 8 September 1965 when it was damaged beyond repair at Istres, again killing its pilot (an American).

Forward propulsion for the Mirage IIIV was to be provided by a single SNECMA TF106 turbofan of 9,000kg (19,842lb), of which a non-afterburning development version, the TF104B of 4,725kg (10,417lb), flew in Mirage IIIT No 01 on 4 June 1964 with Jean Coreau as pilot. The TF104B was a modified version of the US Pratt & Whitney JTF10 (US military TF30) subsonic turbofan and demanded a bulged rear fuselage which was

Left:
Fitted with eight Rolls-Royce RB.108 lift engines and a Bristol Orpheus for forward flight, the VTOL Balzac V prepared the way for the Mirage IIIV. The Balzac gained the rare and unhappy distinction of killing two of its pilots in separate incidents.

Below left:
The General Electric TF106 reheated turbofan was tested in the sole Mirage IIIT. Note the distended rear fuselage.

Bottom:
Chained to the ground for an early test run of its eight RB.162s, Mirage IIIV-01 is pictured unpainted, shortly after roll-out at Melun-Villaroche.

retained when the same trials aircraft flew with the TF106 on 25 January 1965. It remained in use for development work until 1970. A two-seat Mirage IIIT2 was proposed as an equipment testbed, but was not built.

France had meanwhile set great store by the Mirage IIIV and was determined to see it enter Armée de l'Air service, whether or not it won the NATO competition. It transpired that the aircraft was named joint winner with the Hawker P.1154, giving no clear guideline to Treaty members as to which aircraft to buy. The outcome of this indecision was that some countries continued to pursue their own programmes until, eventually, all except Britain lost interest — and even then, the

experimental P.1127 had to be militarised when the P.1154 was axed. As early as 1963 the French Defence Minister was saying that because the Mirage IIIV cost six times more than an IIIE, orders would be limited to a small number for tactical nuclear strike squadrons.

Fitted with eight Rolls-Royce RB.162s of 4,409lb (2,000kg) thrust and a single TF104B, the IIIV-01 was considerably larger than its forebear, with a span of 8.72m (28ft 7.25in), length 18m (59ft 0.5in) and height 5.55m (18ft 2.5in). Tipping the scales at 12,000kg (26,455lb), it was the world's heaviest VTOL fighter. The initial free vertical flight was made by Rene Bigand at Melun-Villaroche on 12 February 1965 and a transition followed at Istres on 24 March 1966. With several detail changes, including revised air intakes, No 02 was forward-powered by an afterburning Pratt & Whitney JTF10 and flew at Melun-Villaroche on 22 June 1966, achieving Mach 2.04 on 12 September the same year. Glory was short-lived, for it crashed at Istres on 28 November.

A year earlier it had been reported that the Mirage IIIV was to be shelved 'temporarily' and the Mirage IIIF-2 developed as a stop-gap. Therefore, it came as no surprise that a replacement was not ordered for IIIV-02 and the programme allowed to lapse. A very different aircraft from first-generation Mirages, the IIIF more properly belongs to the third chapter of this book.

One further Mirage III variant worthy of comment is the Dassault Milan (Kite), whose main characteristic was a pair of retractable foreplanes — rapidly dubbed 'moustaches' — of 1m (39.25in) length astride the nose. Fitted with leading-edge fixed slats and fixed slotted trailing-edge flaps, these devices were developed in conjunction with FFA (the Swiss Federal Aircraft Factory) to impart improved low-speed handling and a better short-field performance.

There were three moustachioed Mirages, of which the first was an embargoed Mirage 5J with foreplanes which could only be adjusted on the ground in 10° steps. This undertook its test programme between September 1968 and March 1969. The next, fully modified, was converted from IIIR No 344 and first flew on 24 May 1969, completing its trials on 10 June, whilst the definitive aircraft, the Milan S (for 'Suisse'), was powered by an Atar 09K-50 and derived from IIIE No 589. Equipped, in addition, with an advanced nav/attack system, its maiden flight was on 29 May 1970 with Guy Mitaux-Maurouard in command, and though it demonstrated a creditable reduction of 12% in landing speed, the Swiss eventually decided against buying more Mirages and turned to the Northrop F-5E instead.

Israel's earlier associations with the Mirage have already been recounted, but when France placed an embargo on delivery of 50 Mirage 5s for the IDF/AF and spares for the existing fleet of IIICJs, steps were taken to acquire the information necessary to produce an almost identical aircraft. As an urgent first step, however, IAI (Israel Aircraft Industries) launched project 'Salvo' involving the re-build to 'zero-hours' condition of battle-weary IIICJs with local components and avionics. What spares could not be produced in Israel were acquired from the US.

This effort led directly to the IAI Nesher (Eagle), a copy of the Mirage 5J retaining the Atar 09C powerplant. The aircraft flew in prototype form during September 1969, and between the start of deliveries in 1972 and the Yom Kippur War of October 1973, some 40 had been supplied, fitted with an air-to-ground optimised radar. Production probably was equivalent to the 50 embargoed aircraft, although some sources put the total as high as 80. In mid-1978 36 Neshers (believed to be all those surviving) were bought by Argentina and delivered over the following few months, adopting the new name Dagger. They were accompanied by three Nesher trainers, which are almost certainly part of a batch of Mirage IIIBs delivered to Israel in kit form in about 1972. Six two-seat aircraft are said to have been supplied in this way, but as one has the c/n T-07, the number could have been higher.

IAI's target, known as 'Black Curtain', was to replace the Atar with a more powerful General Electric J79-J1E of 17,900lb (8,120kg) afterburning thrust, to which end a French-built Mirage (reportedly a IIIB) was persuaded to accept the new powerplant and first flew on 19 October 1970. It was followed by a more representative prototype when a Nesher airframe flew on J79 power in September 1971. The most obvious change necessary to the well-known Mirage shape was a rear fuselage shorter in length, but of greater diameter, and this was clearly apparent in the definitive IAI Kfir (Lion Cub) which flew in 1973. Internal equipment was different from the original Dassault product to such an extent that the Kfir could be regarded almost as another aircraft.

First revealed to the world on 14 April 1975, when the first two were handed-over to the IDF/AF, the Kfir was rapidly updated with the addition of detachable canard foreplanes on the air intake trunks, and other detail changes, under the new designation, Kfir C2 (for 'canard'). These additional surfaces, plus a pair of small nose strakes and a dog-tooth wing leading edge, improve the basic Mirage design substantially, giving better entry to manoeuvres and sustained turning performance, reduced gust sensitivity at all operational altitudes (low level especially) and improved take-off and landing characteristics. Canards — like the Milan's moustaches — largely overcome one of the main deficiencies of a tail-less delta: poor lift at speeds below 240km/hr (150mph), and a configuration unsuited to the addition of high-lift devices. Apart from a disadvantage in close-in combat, this limitation also affects take-off, when raising the trailing edge elevons to lift the nose has the additional and undesirable effect of increasing the effective weight.

Both the Kfir and Kfir C2 exist in interceptor and ground-attack models, the former with the Israeli Elta EL/M2001B radar in an extended nose and the latter featuring a small radar ranging unit. Requirements for a two-seat trainer have been met following the February 1981 first flight of the Kfir TC2, whilst in 1983 deliveries began of the Kfir C7 with its improved avionics and uprated engine and the basically similar TC7 trainer. Canard Kfirs have been sold to Colombia and Ecuador, whilst production for IDF/AF use is expected to end in 1986 after approximately 250 aircraft of all Kfir variants. Strength will steadily decline thereafter, but some 100 will still be in use in 1995.

Above:
Powered by an Atar 9K-50, the Mirage Milan S was tailored to meet a Swiss requirement, but the order went instead to the Northrop F-5E Tiger II.

Below:
Foreplanes — quickly dubbed 'Moustaches' — were a method of improving the Mirage III's slow-speed handling. One of the trials aircraft was Mirage IIIR No 344, which was the first with retractable fitments.

2 The Mirage IV

Bomber Big Brother

Despite the tremendous progress made by France in all areas of human endeavour in the 10 years since the end of World War 2, there remained the feeling that in military affairs the country was still a second-rate power. The United States, Soviet Union and Britain all possessed nuclear weapons and airborne delivery systems, and so it became a matter of national honour for France to gain the means to speak as an equal with the 'Big Three'. Thus came into being the Deterrent Force — la Force de Dissuasion — known colloquially as la Force de Frappe: The Strike Force.

Without the help of its NATO allies, and with military funds severely limited by the demands of colonial wars, France persevered with design, development and production of nuclear weapons, their carriers and support infrastructure. This was achieved through devoting a comparatively modest 5-7% of the defence budget to the task, or about 2% of the national budget. Nuclear delivery by manned aircraft was but the first stage in building the strategic deterrent, now including land and submarine-launched missiles to complement the fleet of bombers produced by Dassault to carry France into the 'nuclear club'.

France's first atomic weapon was detonated in the Sahara on 13 February 1960, but work on its carrier had begun four years before when the Direction Technique et Industrielle de l'Air (Air Technical and Industrial Directorate) received instructions from Président du Conseil, Guy Mollet, to initiate studies of a supersonic bomber.

A two-stage programme was envisaged, the first of which would involve a one-way (or, more accurately, a one-and-a-half-way) aircraft capable of attacking Soviet industrial targets from French airfields and then landing at the nearest NATO base. Having a range of over 3,000km (1,860 miles), this aircraft would penetrate low-level at high subsonic speed before climbing for a Mach 2 sprint attack. Stage two demanded a supersonic bomber three times the size and was soon determined to be beyond technical and financial resources. It was dropped in favour of providing in-flight refuelling facilities for the smaller aircraft — hence the purchase of 12 Boeing C-135F tankers for the Armée de l'Air, replacing the Vautours previously earmarked for support.

Dassault was awarded a design responsibility for the nuclear bomber in April 1957 and was able to make rapid progress through the simple expedient of scaling-up the Mirage III — development of which was well in hand. The resulting Mirage IV emerged with dimensions increased by about 1.5 times, double the wing area, twice the gross weight, and powered by two afterburning Atar 09Bs of 6,000kg (13,210lb) thrust. It was a convenient short-cut to the nuclear club — almost a side entrance — different in many respects from the far more laborious process by which Britain achieved its first-generation nuclear deterrent.

Having a similar 60° swept delta wing to the Mirage III, the bomber was able to make use of more advanced design and structural techniques

Left:
The same, but different. Family likeness is easily seen in an early photograph of the Mirage IVA (left) and Mirage IIIE.

Above:
The unique Mirage IV No 01 differed
from its successors in several respects,
the most obvious of which was the fin
shape. Unfortunately this historic,
record-breaking aircraft was lost in
an accident during 1963.

Left:
The second of the big Mirages, IVA
No 02, was first airborne on 12
October 1961 and is now preserved
in the Musée de l'Air at le Bourget.

Below left:
Fitted with an aerodynamic replica
of the French nuclear bomb semi-
recessed in the fuselage, No 02 makes
a spectacular demonstration of JATO.

Below:
Although assembled at Bordeaux,
Mirage IVAs (like their smaller
relations) took recognisable shape
in the fuselage shop at Argenteuil,
a suburb of Paris.

Above:
Above:
Navigation system trials were undertaken by Mirage IVA No 03, seen here in later configuration with in-flight refuelling probe fitted.

because of its increased dimensions. The result was a wing (produced by Sud Aviation) with a thickness/chord ratio of between 3.8% and 3.2% and milled and tapered solid skins covering almost 95% of the structure weight. Such a system allows integral wing tanks to carry a maximum of fuel — yet the requirement for range was so great that the fin was also constructed (by Breguet) as an integral tank. From the Mirage III also came the system of split elevon control (without inner trimming surface, however) having duplicated power operation and no manual reversion.

Dassault-designed electro-hydraulic controls were tested in the systems mock-up to such effect that no adjustment was found necessary during the first four sorties of the prototype Mirage IV. In addition to power controls, the hydraulic system also operates the air intake centre-bodies, undercarriage and the air brakes mounted above and below the wing in Mirage III fashion. Emergency power is provided by Marquardt ram-jet turbines. There are similarities in fuselage profile between the first two Mirage variants, though the scaled-up aircraft features a systems operator behind the pilot with only two small side windows to provide him with an external view.

Crew comfort is provided for by an air conditioning system for both cockpits, maintaining a steady 20°C despite the kinetic heating effects of comparatively long periods flying at Mach 1.8. Pressurisation is accomplished by an engine bleed-off which also powers the automatic fuel transfer in flight, and there are two engine-driven alternators of 20kVA output. External features of production aircraft include an under-fuselage recess for the AN.22 nuclear store of 60 kiloton, or a similarly-shaped reconnaissance pod; a flattened dome of the CSF mapping radar immediately ahead of the weapon position; and wing attachment points for two groups of six JATO bottles providing rocket-assisted take-off.

Construction of a prototype Mirage IV by Dassault's experimental section at St Cloud was the subject of a preliminary contract of 1 April 1958, this being preceded by two mock-ups for structure and systems installation. Mirage IV-01 was delivered to Melun-Villaroche for final assembly around Christmas of the same year and began hydraulic tests early in 1959. By June, test pilot Roland Galavany was making 'hops' of up to 3,000ft on the 9,200ft runway, and with all ready, No 01 made an initial 40min flight on the morning of 17 June 1959, reaching 325kt (600km/hr) and 11,800ft before landing at 170kt (315km/hr) with the assistance of its 'half-ribbon' drag 'chute. Touch-down speed on this occasion was high as a precautionary measure, the norm soon being established at 140kt (260km/hr).

Unusually, the second sortie included a fly-past — with a Mirage IIIA for scale — at the Paris Air Show. Even more remarkable, demonstrations kept the aircraft occupied until the end of July when, on the eighth flight, it resumed the business of trials and exceeded Mach 1 for the first time. The first target was Mach 1.9 at below 40,000ft (to protect the pilot in case of an accident involving explosive decompression), and after this was achieved during the 14th flight, Rene Bigand took-over the Phase Two testing following Glavany's departure from Dassault. Flights 15 to 27 constituted this part of the programme in which the entire performance envelope was explored up to 59,000ft and three sorties were made by Cdt Marias of the CEV.

The next step was to fit a replica of the nuclear weapon and 550gal (2,500litre) fuel tanks beneath the wings, but the most obvious change during a factory rework at the end of Phase Two was clipping the fin-tip to give the now well-known flat-topped appearance and relocation of the rudder jacks from inside the fuselage to half-way up the fin. In this more representative configuration, No 01 entered Phase Three and achieved Mach 2 on the 33rd sortie (1 December 1959) and demonstrated a cruise speed of Mach 1.85 at 59,000ft, though it was not until after passing these milestones that it first flew with two-seats occupied, on 9 December 1959 with Lucien Martin

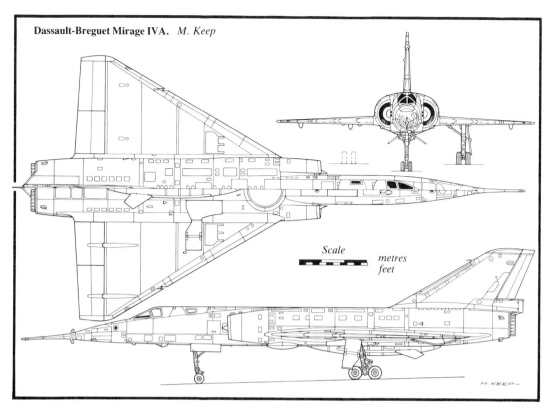

Dassault-Breguet Mirage IVA. *M. Keep*

Scale

metres
feet

M. KEEP—

in the rear position. On 15 December, after repositioning at Istres, the aircraft made its first night flight, soon afterwards completing the third stage of tests with the 42nd sortie. The next part of the programme comprised only two flights to examine aerodynamic characteristics after weapon release (ie, with the recess open to the airflow). By February 1960, after temporary return to Dassault just prior to the start of official trials at the CEV, No 01 had sustained Mach 1.7 at 50,000ft for 38 minutes during one sortie.

No 01 was delivered to the CEV at Istres on 19 February in the course of its 52nd flight and performed so well that the specified testing was completed by 15 September 1960, when it was reverted to Dassault. The priority was now to take the 1,000km closed-circuit record, a feat accomplished in two traverses of a 502km course around Paris flown at 1,820km/hr (1,130.9mph) between 40,000 and 50,000ft. The award-winning prototype remained a company trials aircraft until destroyed in an accident on 13 December 1963.

The loss had little effect on the development programme, for three pre-series aircraft had flown by that time and the initial production model was taking shape. No 02 was the first Mirage IVA and undertook its maiden flight on 12 October 1961 powered by two 6,400kg (14,110lb) thrust Atar 09Cs. It was slightly larger than No 01, with span

increased almost half a metre to 11.85m (38ft 10.5in) and a wing area of 78sq m (840sq ft). Fitted with an under-fuselage radome, it spent its early life at Colomb Bechar in the Algerian Sahara on bombing trials and is now an exhibit at the Musée de l'Air, Le Bourget.

No 03 took to the air on 1 June 1962 and specialised in development of the navigation system which, apart from CSF radar, includes Marconi Doppler, a Dassault computer and countermeasures equipment and a SFENA auto-pilot. Though initially fitted with a pitot in the nose, it later exchanged this for a flight-refuelling probe and was engaged in trials with a C-135F tanker. Its last remains — the fin and an undercarriage leg — were to be seen preserved at the Chateaudun maintenance unit as late as 1983.

Finally, No 04 was flown in full production form on 23 January 1963, complete with Atar 09K engines of 7,000kg (15,400lb) thrust and the full range of operational equipment. Production then turned immediately to the 50 ordered in 1960, of which the first was flown at Bordeaux, the manufacturing centre for series aircraft, on 7 December 1963. A further 12 were ordered later to provide reserves for attrition replacement, and in less than a year the first squadron of Mirage IVAs was on round-the-clock alert. France was the world's fourth nuclear power.

France's national strategic force, now including long-range missles launched from land and beneath the sea, began to take shape a month after the first production Mirage IVA had flown. In the unlikely setting of a hilltop near Taverny, just northwest of Paris, the Commandement des Forces Aériennes Stratégiques (CoFAS) was established on 1 January 1964, ready to administer a fast-flowing equipment programme.

Externally, Base Aérienne 921, Taverny, is but a small collection of buildings and communications antennae, yet deep underground is the nerve-centre of deterrent forces operated by the Armée de l'Air. Also in 'le Trou' (the Hole) is the HQ of Air Defence Command, ensuring maximum co-operation between the two most vital Armée de l'Air elements. Like the Mirage IVA bases and their nuclear weapon stocks, Taverny is a well-guarded installation whose secrets are kept secure. However, there was to be no disguising the formation of the FAS, for its effects were profound. At last possessing the means to defend itself against all possible aggressors, France (in the person of President de Gaulle) announced on 10 March 1966 that it would leave the military side of NATO.

For the next few months, there was considerable interchange of units as French forces withdrew from West Germany and some Canadian and US elements, together with the NATO headquarters, vacated French soil. There were many who said that France had gone too far and seriously weakened the Alliance by its new 'tous azimuts' (all directions) policy, which declined to nominate any one country or power group as a potential aggressor and maintained that sovereignty could be threated from any sector. Thus, for a while, it was politically acceptable for the French and Soviet air forces to make annual courtesy visits to each other's airfields.

Initial Mirage IVA deliveries were made to Mont-de-Marsan during 1964 and following crew training with the Centre d'Expérimentations Aériennes Militaires, the first squadron was simultaneously established and declared oper-ational at the same base on 1 October. The deployment plan called for three escadres (wings) to receive the new nuclear bomber, each of these comprising three squadrons with four aircraft apiece and a refuelling squadron operating four Boeing C-135Fs. One major difference between the AA and its British and US allies was that the FAS was permanently dispersed, with no more than four operational aircraft on any base at any time. This must have increased maintenance costs, compared with (say) the RAF, which had anything up to 30 V-bombers at an airfield and would only send them out in fours to other bases when the political situation began to look grim.

The three escadres (wings) chosen to maintain the airborne deterrent were the 91st, 93rd and 94th — the 92nd was at that time flying Sud Vautour IIBs — and Escadron de Bombardement (EB) 1/91 'Gascogne' had the honour of being first equipped, followed by EB 2/91 'Bretagne' at Cazaux, EB 3/91 'Beauvaisis' at Creil/Senlis and Escadron de Ravitaillement en Vol (ERV) 4/91 'Landes' — the latter an in-flight refuelling squadron formed at Mont-de-Marsan on 1 January 1965. There is, of course, a basic incompatibility between USAF and French refuelling methods, but this was quickly (if not neatly) solved by adding a short length of hose connected to a drogue on to the end of the C-135F's 'flying boom'.

There was hardly a pause before the 93e Escadre de Bombardement was re-formed with EB 1/93 'Guyenne' and ERV 4/93 'Aunis' both at Istres, EB 2/93 'Cévennes' at Orange and EB 3/93 'Sambre' at Cambrai. Finally it was the turn of 94

Left:
Bordeaux in the early 1960s would reveal intense activity in the Mirage IVA final assembly hangar. Nearest the camera are Nos 22, 24 and 25.

wing: EB 1/94 'Bourbonnais' and ERV 4/94 'Sologne' at Avord, EB 2/94 'Marne' at St Dizier and EB 3/94 'Arbois' at Luxeuil. 'Arbois' formed on 1 February 1966, though it was not until November that the 62nd and last Mirage IVA was received. Of these, 36 were constantly on line and the remainder allocated to training, or second-line servicing at Bordeaux by the AA echelon, Groupe D'Entretien et de Réparation des Matériels Spécialisés (GERMaS) 15/96.

Consequently aircraft were regularly moved from unit to unit and so partly for this reason (and presumably for security too) squadron or wing insignia were not applied to the bare metal airframes except temporarily for special occasions. As a further deception, Mirage IVAs used peacetime radio call-signs in the range reserved for AA Training Command (F-THAA onwards), the last two of which were eventually applied in large characters on the nose. The sequence was straightforward, with Nos 2-62 becoming AA to CI in sequence, while released from its trials use, No 1 was painted as AP to fill the gap caused by the early demise (5 June 1966) of No 17.

At first, wings had their own training and communications fleet of Mirage IIIBs, Lockheed T-33As and Dassault Flamants, but the situation was soon changed when the Centre d'Instruction des FAS (CIFAS 328) formed at Bordeaux and began receiving specialist equipment. In addition to the 'regular' Mirage IIIB came the IIIB-RV with its dummy refuelling probe, and Nord 2501SNB Noratlases fitted with bulbous noses carrying the Mirage IVA's Système de Navigation et de Bombardement for navigator training. The T-33s (replaced in 1982-83 by Fouga Magisters and DB/D Alpha Jets) and Noratlases are operated by Escadron 3/328, whilst the Mirage IIIs came under Escadron D'Entrainement 2/328. Four Mirage IVAs, which may be fitted with a recce pod constitute Escadron de Reconnaissance et d'Instruction 1/328.

The FAS was the elite of the French armed forces and received priority in all things. On the ground, each Mirage IVA base had a Dépôt-Atelier de Munitions Spéciales (DAMS) to store, maintain and assemble the 65 kiloton free-fall bomb, and its installations and the aircraft's blast-proof hangars were closely guarded by (it is alleged) a particularly hardened breed of Gen-

Right:
Early production Mirage IVAs involved in the trials programme.

Below:
Mirage IVA No 1, photographed at Bordeaux immediately before its first flight, shows the shape of the dummy nuclear store protruding from the fuselage lines.

Above:
France's airborne strategic nuclear force was completed by a dozen Boeing C-135F tankers. For compatibility with the Mirage IVA's probe refuelling system, they carry a drogue 'basket' on a short length of hose at the end of the USAF-style 'flying boom'.

Above right:
Equipped with a CT52 reconnaissance pod in place of the nuclear weapon, a Mirage IVA of CIFAS 328 lifts off from the Bordeaux runway at the start of a sortie.

darmerie de l'Air and Commandos de l'Air. A Mirage IVA first dropped a nuclear weapon at Mururoa Atoll, 800 miles (1,300km) southeast of Tahiti, in July 1966, this being a trial free-fall device of 18 kilotons which exploded at low level. In the following year it was announced that the FAS would be equipped with modified bombs incorporating a parachute retarding system, and these entered service soon afterwards, in the second half of 1967. By 1973 the latest AN.22 weapon was in use, still with a yield of 65 kilotons but its weight halved to about 750kg (1,650lb).

The retarded method of delivery indicated that after a two-year study France was following the RAF's V-Force in going 'under the radar' to minimise the risk of detection and interception, at which height a parachute was required to stop the bomb rebounding. Minor modifications for the low-level role, such as some structural beefing-up and changes to the controls and avionics, were embodied in the Mirage IVA, although application of green and grey camouflage appropriate to the new operating height did not begin until 1975, starting with No 4.

Crew requirements also received priority, for the initial deployment plan involved 12 aircraft constantly airborne, 12 at 4min readiness, and 12 at 45min. This placed an immense strain on the support organisation — not to mention airframes

— and so until 1975, when it was further relaxed, the stipulation was one aircraft from each of the nine squadrons available for take-off in 15min. In the early days of the FAS, however, crews were flying some 25 hours per month and aircraft were sometimes aloft for up to 14 hours on a single sortie, thanks to C-135F tankers (whose pilots were flying 30 hours per month). During its first 10 years of service, the Mirage IVA fleet flew almost 200,000 hours and achieved some 40,000 mid-air refuellings.

Even as the Mirage IVA force was building up, an unusual export prospect emerged just across the Channel. On 6 April 1965 Britain's government axed the British Aircraft Corporation (BAC) TSR-2 strike aircraft development programme and began looking for a cheaper replacement. BAC joined with Dassault in promoting a 'Mirage IV*' powered by two 21,000lb (9,525kg) thrust Rolls-Royce Spey 25R reheated turbofans and fitted with TSR-2 avionics including the nav/attack and terrain-avoidance systems, plus an optional reconnaissance pod. Priced at £1.5 to £1.6million each for a UK-assembled run of 75-80 aircraft (or less if the projected 140 were purchased) the revamped Mirage IV* was £1million cheaper than its American rival, the General Dynamics F-111.

The RAF was less than enthusiastic and preferred the F-111, whilst watching price estimates of the Anglo-French aircraft increase to £2million in January 1966 and at least £2.2million by the following month. Nevertheless, it was considered that the Mirage IV* could meet most of the RAF's demands and would be both strong enough and have the right gust-response characteristics for high-speed flight at 200ft (61m). Deliveries were planned to begin in 1969, given a decision to proceed late in 1965. Externally the aircraft would have been characterised by a 2ft (0.61m) fuselage extension immediately forward of the air intakes and an increase of fuselage depth by 3in (0.076m) — both in connection with the extra weight and size of the Spey engines. When the Government did decide on the TSR-2's replacement, the Defence White Paper of 22 February 1966 revealed that the F-111 had been chosen. The Mirage IV* was thus stillborn — as, ironically, was the British F-111K: the escalating price and delayed delivery was too much for the Government, which eventually bought the HS Buccaneer, which had been on offer all the time.

Back in France, missiles were now available to back the Mirage IVA, and so a scaling-down of the force was ordered, officially effective from 1 June 1976. Three escadrons disappeared in the move, which also took the opportunity to collect the C-135Fs in one wing and shuffle some unit identities so that senior squadrons remained in being. The two Mirage IVA-only wings were EB 91 and EB 94, whilst ERV 93 managed the 11 surviving tankers, the squadrons now being EB 1/91 'Gascogne' at Mont-de-Marsan, EB 2/91 'Bretagne' at Cazaux, EB 3/91 'Cévennes' at Orange, EB 1/94 'Guyenne' at Avord, EB 2/94 'Marne' at St Dizier, EB 3/94 'Arbois' at Luxeuil, ERV 1/93 'Aunis' at Istres, ERV 2/93 'Landes' at Mont-de-Marsan and ERV 3/93 'Sologne' at Avord.

Four aircraft, operated by CIFAS 328, were assigned to the long-range reconnaissance role, for which a total of 12 Mirage IVAs was modified with the fittings to carry a 1,000kg (2,200lb) CT 52 recce pod in the same position as the nuclear weapon. Five CT 52s were delivered in 1977, each containing vertical, oblique and forward cameras such as three high-altitude Omera 36s and three low-level Omera 35s, plus a single Wildt mapping camera. Alternative fitments in the CT 52 included trials of a SAT Super Cyclope low-level infra-red system in place of the Omera 36s.

Re-organisation came at a time when France was rethinking its defensive strategy. Like NATO, it had abandoned the tripwire policy of all-out nuclear retaliation to any aggressive act by the Warsaw Pact, and it was also coming closer to the Alliance — on a different, though parallel, road. Tacitly admitting that the main, if not only, danger lay in the east, Chief of General Staff Gen Guy Mery summed it up when he said, 'It would be extremely dangerous for us to remain out of that first battle in which our own security would be at stake'. Therefore, NATO took it as read that France would fight with the rest of the Western powers and not wait until Warsaw Pact soldiers arrived at Strasbourg.

The diminished force of 24 operational Mirage IVAs which would have been hastily re-integrated in the NATO battle plan was due to disband in 1985, though some aircraft would have remained in the recce role for longer. However, part of the fleet was granted a new lease of life as the result of

Aérospatiale being awarded a development and roduction order in April 1978 for its ASMP (Air-Sol Moyenne Portée) 100-150 kiloton nuclear stand-off weapon. Primarily intended to be carried by the Mirage 2000N and Super Etendard, the ASMP is a supersonic missile powered by a kerosene-burning ramjet, guided to its target at low level by an inertial navigation system with terrain-following capability. Range is reportedly up to 100km (62 miles).

In 1979 it was announced that 15 (later increased to 18) Mirage IVAs would be converted to carry a single ASMP, 5.38m (17ft 8in) long, on a new centreline pylon, and equipped with Antilope 5 ground-mapping radar, a new inertial navigation system and other detail changes for compatibility with the advanced weapon. The designation was at first notified as IVN (for Nucléaire), though later amended to IVP, indicating Pénétration in the hi-lo-hi mode up to a radius of 4,000km (2,500 miles) with in-flight refuelling. Late in 1984, however, mention of Antilope was dropped, and without fanfare the Mirage IVP's radar was stated to be the Thomson-CSF ARCANA. Indicating Appareil de Récalage et de Cartographie pour Navigation Aveugle, ARCANA is derived from the Iguane and VARAN systems used by the Atlantique 2 and Gardian respectively, and is a pulse-Doppler with high-resolution mapping capability in all weathers.

First trials for the new programme were undertaken by the aged Mirage IVA prototype, No 03, whose centre fuselage was used for static tests of the ASMP's pylon and release mechanism at Chateaudun. Mirage IVA No 8 was next selected as the prototype IVP, but first, in unconverted form during 1981, it was used as an aerodynamic and mechanical testbed, dropping free-fall ASMPs during operations from CEV, Cazaux. No 4 was also brought in soon afterwards, this Mirage IVA making the first four live ASMP launches, beginning in June 1983. By October 1982, No 8 had been converted to the new standard — apart from the ECM equipment — by Dassault and repainted as IVP No 01, and it was handed over to the CEAM at Mont-de-Marsan on 1 July 1983 for operational trials. Assessment was by a 15-man team of officers and NCOs, led by a FAS navigator in deference to the many avionics changes in the 'P' model. Later in 1983, when the following year's defence allocations were announced, it became known that conversion of the first seven IVAs would be funded, followed by the release of cash for the remaining 11 in 1985.

A second aircraft, the former IVA No 28, flew in May 1983 as IVP No 02, its duties including ground testing, such as ECM trials in Dassault's anechoic chamber at Istres, estimation of maintenance requirements, and weapon safety checks by

Dassault at Cuers — the later including proof-testing against the effects of electromagnetic pulses using CEAT's mobile generator. This work kept it grounded for some time, so that by the end of 1984 No 02 had flown on some 70 occasions, compared with the total of 250 hours achieved up to the same time by No 01 in missions on behalf of Dassault and the CEV (both at Istres) and CEAM. No 01 took over ASMP firings from IVA No 4, and by early 1985 had undertaken four test launches and one of the planned three qualification tests. Investigation also has been made of remaining fatigue life, in the absence of a long-term programme — originally thought unnecessary for the short life at high altitude imagined during the early days of service. An ultimate life limitation of 7,500 hours is thought probable, but with main spar replacement at 6,500 hours, and although many aircraft are now approaching 5,000 hours, there are sufficient main spars currently in stock to ensure the fleet's continued operation.

The AA is handling its own Mirage IVP conversion programme, with work undertaken at the Atelier Industriel de l'Air at Aulnat/Clermont-Ferrand, to which the first subject was delivered in October 1983. As IVP No 1, it was rolled out in December 1984 and delivered to CEAM in mid-February 1985. Although completely over-hauled and re-wired, this and the next three were not fully representative of Service standard and were due to be returned for minor updating, beginning late the same year. From IVP No 5, in September 1985, deliveries of fully-modified aircraft will continue until No 17 is complete in mid-1977, following which No 02 will have its test instrumentation removed to complete the force of 18 operational aircraft.

Issue to front-line units will take place in 1986, and only two squadrons are to fly the Mirage IVP, these sharing about 15 aircraft, whilst the CIFAS at Bordeaux has the rest for training. EB 91 is the designated operator, and, following disbandment of EB 3/91 'Cévennes' on 1 October 1983, it seems likely that EB 1/91 'Gascogne' and EB 2/91 'Bretagne' will be the units to fly the Mirage IVP/ASMP combination. Having disbanded its third squadron in 1983, EB 94 was flying two units of AN.22-armed Mirage IVAs in 1985, but with retirement imminent. Not until 1996, when a new ICBM — currently known as the SX — becomes operational, will it be time for EB 91 to retire its Mirage IVPs. Completion of 32 years as a strategic nuclear deterrent will be a glowing epitaph for the 'Big Mirage'.

Above:
Wearing the current camouflage scheme, this Mirage IVA is equipped with a Philips-Matra Phimat chaff dispenser on each of the outer wing pylons.

Below:
Using its brake parachute for landing, a Mirage IVA of CIFAS 328. A 2,500litre (550gal) fuel tank is carried on each of the inboard wing pylons.

3 The Mirage F1

The Delta is Dropped

For its second generation of Mirages, Avions Marcel Dassault created a new breed of aircraft far removed in levels of technology from products of the mid-1950s. After a couple of false starts, activities finally came to centre on an aircraft which has been adopted as the standard multi-mission fighter of the home air force and purchased, in addition, by several customers abroad, achieving a current sales total approaching 700. However, before examining in detail how Dassault built success upon success, it will be instructive to look briefly at other products of the St Cloud experimental department in the 1960s.

To say that the Mirage III was 'wrong' from the outset is to deny the evidence of an order book which would be coveted by any aircraft manufac-

turer, yet none appreciated more than Dassault that the delta configuration was an unsatisfactory

Below:
A venture into variable geometry, the Mirage G flew in November 1967, a few months after France abandoned a joint multi-role combat aircraft programme with Britain. Briefly it seemed that the Mirage G might be used as the basis of a unilateral project, but this was not to be.

Bottom:
The major contribution made by the Mirage IIIF2 to Mirage evolution was in the new wing — mounted high on the fuselage and accompanied by a low-set tailplane. Nothing came of the two-seat IIIF2, yet when scaled down it proved to be another winning design.

Although the Mirage III/5 series remained in production for a decade after the Mirage F1 entered service, much floor space at Bordeaux was given over to the new aircraft. Production reached a peak of seven aircraft per month.

compromise. It enabled the Mirage to have a 4% thickness : chord ratio for high-speed performance without resorting to the almost solid, ultra-thin wing which Lockheed chose for the Starfighter, the balancing disadvantages for the French aircraft including less than docile handling at low speed. The perfect solution was a thin wing attached to a fighter of conventional (with tailplane) layout, in which could be included slats, drooped leading edges and double-slotted flaps. Technology to produce such a wing was available by the 1960s, and differing ways in which it might be employed were foreseen.

In the VTOL Mirage Balzac and IIIV we have already looked at one of the two principal aerodynamic fads of the 1960s; the other was variable geometry, 'swing wings'. On 17 May 1965, a month after the TSR-2 was cancelled, Britain signed a Memorandum of Understanding with France concerning development of a combat aircraft known as the AFVG (Anglo-French Variable Geometry). BAC and Dassault were to produce the airframe, and Rolls-Royce and SNECMA, the engine, work with the former being

assisted by a contract placed with Dassault on 13 October 1965 for a VG aircraft to be known as the Mirage G.

A two-seat design, the Mirage G was sufficiently complete for static display at Melun-Villaroche late in May 1967 (during the Paris Air Show), though it did not leave the ground, at Istres, until 18 November, powered by a single 9,000kg (19,840lb) thrust SNECMA TF-306 afterburning turbofan. Meanwhile, on 29 June 1967, the AFVG had been abandoned in a unilateral announcement by the French Government, which for a while afterward toyed with the idea of using the Mirage G as the basis of an operational aircraft. Trials began well, the aircraft covering the complete range of wing sweep (from 25° to 70°) within a week of its maiden flight and reaching Mach 2.1 after two months. Weighing half as much again, empty, as a Mirage IIIE, the 'G' landed 40km/hr (25mph) slower in a convincing demonstration of its leading and trailing-edge flaps.

After 316 sorties and some 400 hours in the air, Mirage G No 001 crashed on 13 January 1971 (test pilot René Bigand making a safe escape) and was replaced in the development programme by two Mirage G8s. Each powered by a pair of 7,200kg (15,870lb) thrust Atar 9K50s pending availability of the definitive 8,500kg (18,740lb) SNECMA M53s, the G8s were clearly intended as prototypes of a new line of deep-penetration aircraft and featured Cyrano IV multi-purpose radar, a low-altitude nav/attack system including laser ranger, Doppler, and a bombing computer. No 01 first flew on 8 May 1971 and reached Mach 2.02 on its fourth flight, just four days later, whilst No 02 joined it in the air on 13 July 1972. The historic G8 No 01 is now preserved by the Musée de l'Air.

The G8 was a late competitor to the MRCA (later Tornado) and would have come to the fore if this trinational programme had faltered. When it did not, and France determined its main requirement to be for a fixed-geometry air superiority type, it was recast in 1972 as the Mirage G8A, or ACF (Avion de Combat Futur), with a 55° swept wing. Weighing about 14,000kg (30,900lb), the single-seat G8A/ACF would have been in the Mach 3 class, though further changes of requirements resulted in its cancellation in 1975 before a prototype could be completed. It thus joined two other derivatives which were abandoned in 1970: the single-seat Mirage G2 carrier-based naval fighter and Mirage G4 22,700kg (50,040lb) gross weight two-seat bomber — a prototype of which was partially built.

Parallel with this line of development, Dassault had been working on fixed-geometry Mirages and, indeed, the original Mirage G had a fuselage almost identical to the sole Mirage F2 — first known as the IIIF2. The F2 began life as an officially-sponsored testbed for the SNECMA TF-306 turbofan (which was to power the Mirage IIIV) when it was found that the Mirage IIIT — specifically built for the task — could not perform at the lower end of the speed spectrum. Trying to be as like the IIIT as possible, the F2 differed radically in that the delta was foresaken in favour of a high wing and low tailplane.

The advantages of this layout and the improved wing it made possible were soon apparent. F2 No 01 first flew on 12 June 1966, sustained by a Pratt & Whitney TF-30 because its TF-306 was not available, and on 29 December the same year it exceeded Mach 2 for the first time, before landing in a mere 1,575ft (480m). Though sponsored by the air force as a possible operational combat aircraft which would fill the gap between Mirage IIIs and the variable-geometry aircraft which were to have been available in the mid-1970s, the F2 was not developed and its airframe is now preserved at Toulouse. A single-seat air superiority version of the F2 — provisionally designated Mirage F3 — was briefly considered early in 1967, but failed to progress beyond the drawing board.

Meanwhile, as a private venture, and with a follow-on to the Mirage III/5 in mind, Dassault scaled-down the F2 to about first-generation Mirage size and fitted the resulting aircraft with an uprated Atar 9K engine. This smaller model retained its companion's full range of high lift devices and showed that it could operate from semi-prepared strips only 2,625ft (800m) long at typical combat mission weight. Cyrano radar provided interception capability with a secondary air-to-ground role, and in combination these attributes were deemed to be just what the Armée de l'Air wanted. This then was to be the new French multi-mission fighter, and it was called the Mirage F1.

Below:
The obligatory weapon options photograph stresses the continued versatility of the Mirage line.

The Mirage F1 Described

The private-venture design which began as the Mirage III-E2 in mid-1964 and was later known as III-F1 bore the inscription 'Mirage F1C' on the nose when René Bigand lifted it off from the runway at Melun-Villaroche on 23 December 1966. In an early demonstration of its potential as a Mirage III replacement No 01, again with Bigand in command, exceeded Mach 2 during its fourth sortie (on the afternoon of 7 January 1967), then touched down at a comparatively docile 222km/hr (138mph) to stress the speed range of what was now being termed the 'Super Mirage F-1'. This was achieved on the 6,600kg (14,700lb) reheated thrust (4,700kg/10,350lb dry) of an Atar 9K turbojet, and would obviously be improved in time.

Sadly, though, time ran out for the Mirage F1 and Dassault's respected Chief Test Pilot sooner than expected: having positioned to Istres for the 44-year old Bigand to rehearse his display sequence for the coming Paris Air Show, No 01 broke-up in mid-air at Fos, near Marseilles, on 18 May in the course of its 24th flight. It was a serious blow, but not one which would affect the programme, because the decision had already been taken to develop the Mirage F1 for Armée de l'Air use.

In January 1967, Armed Forces Minister Pierre Messmer had revealed that although the AA was well equipped with tactical and ground-attack fighters, it was short on interceptors. Acquisition of 100 Mirage F1s was then revealed to be under

Below:
Though tragically short, the life of the Mirage F1 prototype was sufficient to reveal the promise held by the revised design. Note the radome shape in comparison with subsequent aircraft.

Bottom:
Displaying its leading-edge flaps to advantage, the second F1 takes off on an early test flight, bearing the name 'Super Mirage F1'.

Above:
A slow fly-by of F1-02 with 'everything down'.

serious consideration, with a decision due early in February (by which time the F1 had only completed the first phase of its trials programme, comprising eight sorties). This was confirmed on 26 May when an order for three F1s and a static test airframe was revealed to be in prospect — though it was September before a signature formalised the position. A few months later a further order covered final development work and production drawings.

The key date however was 29 June, when France's departure from the AFVG programme was announced. Dassault had campaigned hard to have the variable geometry combat aircraft dropped, and when the programme collapsed, the available funding was switched to the Mirage F1, assuring its future. (This was not to be the last time that the company was involved in a co-British conflict of interest: representatives of BAe have complained that Dassault-Breguet would discover the identity of potential customers for the Jaguar through its half share in the aircraft, and then persuade them to buy Mirages instead.)

Little secret is made of the fact that official adoption of the Mirage F1 was a political decision. Some history books have been rewritten to show the aircraft as a private-venture response to an official specification calling for a Mirage III replacement. In fact, as we have seen, the F1 owes its origin to the scaling-down of an experimental aircraft which was hastily produced to undertake low-speed trials of a potential VTOL aircraft's engine when the original testbed proved unsatisfactory. It would not be far short of the truth to say that the Mirage F1 was developed by accident — though a most fortuitous one.

There was never any specification for the Mirage F1 until March 1967 (that is to say, after it had flown), and the first production order is said to have been purely a manoeuvre to launch the programme and compensate Dassault for taking over Breguet. With such a background, an ordinary aircraft might have proved to be a disaster, but once it got its hands on the F1, the Armée de l'Air was convinced that that is was what it always wanted.

Almost two years were to elapse before the Mirage F1 could continue the interrupted flight-test programme. The first officially-sponsored aircraft, No 02, was completed at St Cloud in December 1968 and then dismantled for the journey to Istres (the test centre replacing Melun-Villaroche). The task was completed by 20 January, when the aircraft was ready to begin vibration trials, prior to first flight. At this stage power was provided by a 6,700kg (14,770lb) thrust Atar 9K-31B(3) — derived from the 9K-7 fitted in the Mirage IVA — pending availability of the definitive 9K-50.

A couple of weeks behind schedule, on 20 March 1969, Dassault's project test pilot, Jean-Marie Saget, was strapped into No 02 and it took off at the start of a remarkable first flight, lifting-off in 450m (1,475ft). As would be the norm, undercarriage, flaps and airbrakes were tested on this initial sortie, the departure from accepted practice coming when Saget took the aircraft up to Mach 1.15. Landing after 50min in the air, No 02 pulled up in 400m (1,310ft). During the second flight, on the next day, Saget opened another large portion of the flight envelope by achieving Mach 1.5 before bringing No 02 down to 213km/hr (132mph) for slow-speed qualification trials. The approach was made at 250km/hr (155mph) and landing at 232km/hr (144mph).

The second flight had included 5g manoeuvres,

and these were repeated during the third sortie (24 March) at a speed of Mach 1.8. Before it landed, the F1 touched Mach 2.03. Within a month this had been bettered, Chief Test Pilot Jean Coreau winding No 02 up to Mach 2.12 at 36,000ft during its 15th flight (23 April). Earlier in the day the same pilot had manoeuvred at 6g and Mach 1.8 with Sidewinder AAMs on the wingtips. Needless to say, its short-field performance and manoeuvrability were highlights of that year's Paris Salon.

Sixty-two flights, the last in the evening of 27 June, completed Phase One of the Mirage F1's test programme. Achievements in addition to those already mentioned included a flight of over 50,000ft (15,240m); low-altitude operation at 1,300km/hr (808mph); carriage of military loads such as 1,100litre (242gal) tanks beneath each wing; and exploration of the full flight envelope. This was undertaken mainly by Saget and Coureau, assisted by Capt Guillard of the CEV

flight-test centre. After a scheduled lay-up, during which it was fitted with a pre-series version of the Atar 9K-50, No 02 flew again in August.

Development progressed more rapidly after Saget took the 9K-50-powered No 03 aloft at Istres for the first time on 18 September 1969, reaching Mach 1.45 during the 50min flight. Up to then

Below:
Amongst the tasks of Mirage F1-04 were trial firings of the MATRA Super 530 radar-guided AAM, seen here leaving the starboard wing pylon.

Bottom:
The Mirage's 'dogfight' AAM is the MATRA R.550 Magic. A Mk 2 version, as shown, entered service in 1984.

No 02 had flown on 77 occasions, accumulating some 80 hours, and the pair brought the combined total to 120 sorties and 135 hours by the time Phase Two testing was completed in December. No 02 then transferred to CEV, Cazaux, for armament tests which began on 22 December and culminated in completion of cannon-firing trials at CEAM, Mont-de-Marsan, on 27 February. These involved release of 4,000 rounds from the new DEFA 553 weapon at Mach 1.6 in air-to-air mode, and at 1,300km/hr (808mph) air-to-ground. Shortly before this, No 02 had been fitted with a production Atar 9K-50 of 7,160kg (15,785lb) thrust, with which it achieved Mach 2.15 at 53,000ft (16,155m) and sustained a speed in excess of Mach 2 for seven minutes during flights 137 and 138 on 21 February — the former its first with the new engine.

Fitment of the under-fuselage MATRA 530 AAM had been made by the time the two aircraft reached a combined total of 200 sorties (11 March 1970, with No 03 contributing 50). Built to production standards, No 04 joined the programme on 17 June 1970, and in August 1971 it was this aircraft which was the subject of interception trials and air-to-ground firing at the CEAM, scoring over 50% despite poor operating conditions. When Dassault test pilot Alan Tretout took No 04 on its 210th flight, on 2 May 1972, it was the 1,000th by the three sponsored Mirage F1s. By that time 47 pilots from the air force, navy, CEV and seven foreign countries had flown the aircraft.

No 04 had the full avionics system and soon adopted the revised wing pioneered by No 03, on which leading edges are extended for a greater proportion of the overall span than was the case with No 02. The wing, with its extensive array of high-lift devices, has been cited earlier as the F1's most valuable asset, and so a closer examination is now in order of this and other important features.

Mirage F1 mainplanes are of an all-metal, two-spar torsion-box structure reliant in large measure on mechanically or chemically milled components. Swept at 47° 30′, they have extended chord (dog tooth) on the outer two-thirds of the leading edge, whilst trailing edge control surfaces are of honeycomb sandwich construction. The entire leading edge may be drooped for take-off and landing (and is operated automatically in combat), and each trailing edge has two differentially-operating double-slotted flaps and one aileron, the last-mentioned compensated by trim devices incorporated in linkage. Spoilers and ailerons are manufactured by Potez. During flight-testing, this new wing reduced take-off distance by 28%, approach speed by 22% and increased manoeuvrability by up to 80% compared with the Mirage III, though with present operational equipment the first two figures have been reduced to 23% and 20% respectively. Light, small and thin, yet very strong, the wing has an area of 25sq m (269.1sq ft), or substantially less than the Mirage III's 35sq m (377sq ft), yet the newcomer has a gross weight 2.5 tonnes greater than the IIIE, at 16,200kg (35,715lb). Part of this is the result of the F1's considerably increased internal fuel capacity: 43% more than the IIIE.

The fuselage is a conventional all-metal semi-monocoque construction in which electrical spot-welding is used for secondary stringers and sealed panels, whilst the remainder of joints are titanium flush riveted or bolted and sealed. A perforated airbrake is located in the forward underside of each intake trunk. Almost all is sub-contracted, the nose and cockpit to Aérospatiale; canopy to SOCEA; part of the centre fuselage to CASA in Spain; rear fuselage to Fairey and SABCA of Belgium; and tail to SOCATA. The tailplane is of the all-moving type, actuated hydraulically by electrical or manual coontrol, and a braking parachute is located in a bullet fairing at the base of the rudder.

A complex folding mechanism is used for the two single mainwheels of the Messier-Hispano-Bugatti tricycle undercarriage, whilst the lower front fuselage houses a pair of DEFA 553 30mm cannon with 135 rounds per gun, firing 50rds/sec at a muzzle velocity of over 800m/sec (2,625ft/sec). The air-conditioned cockpit includes a Martin-Baker F1RM4 ejection seat in early production aircraft or an SEM Martin-Baker F10M rocket seat in newer single-place models. Trainers have Mk10s with inter-related firing, exit in all cases being through the canopy after explosive pre-fragmentation.

As in the Mirage III/5 family, the equipment fit may be varied according to a customer's specification. The baseline (but not most basic) model is the F1C all-weather fighter with its multi-mode Thomson-CSF Cyrano IV fire-control radar in the nose for all-aspect, all-altitude interception. In the F1E this capability is augmented by avionics for undertaking ground attack in all weathers, including air-to-ground mapping and continuous target ranging modes on the Cyrano IV. Additionally, the F1E has a Kearfott 40 inertial platform, a main EMD 182 nav/attack computer,

and a VE-120 cathode ray tube head-up display.

The simpler Mirage F1A carries extra fuel but lacks the Cyrano IV, using instead an EMD AIDA 2 radar (protected by a far smaller radome) for target ranging. It may operate as a day interceptor with infra-red AAMs, though the main role is ground attack, for which it has an SAS (Système d'Attaque au Sol). This comprises a Doppler-effect EMD navigation system, Thompson-CSF laser sighting unit, SFIM inertial central unit, two Crouzet and Thomson-CSF computers, a Thomson-CSF 129 head-up display and a map display by the same firm, and enables the target to be acquired at a distance of 5km (three miles) for automatic bomb release.

Reconnaissance may be undertaken by the addition of a centreline pod or with the internal sensors of the specialised F1CR. Ordered by France, the F1CR is fitted with two optical cameras (a panoramic OMERA 40 and a vertical OMERA 33) and a SAT SCM 2400 Super Cyclope infra-red detector in the cannon bay. The Cyrano IVMR radar is retained, despite earlier plans to fit an advanced unit optimised for ground mapping and attack, and a ULISS 47 INS provides the navigational accuracy demanded in recce missions. Four specialised pods are being developed for centreline carriage: Raphael side-looking airborne radar; ASTAC (Analyseur Super-hétérodyne Tactique) for locating ground radars; HAROLD, permitting long-range, high-resolution photography; and NORA (Nacelle Optique de Reconnaissance Aérienne) for high or low-level work.

Finally, the F1B two-seat trainer retains Cyrano, but loses the integral cannon and some fuel capacity, though is otherwise capable of operational missions. The forward fuselage includes a 30cm (11.8in) extension and empty weight is 200kg (440lb) more than the F1C. Mirage F1 versions equipped with the internal 'plumbing' necessary for installation of a removable in-flight refuelling probe on the starboard side of the nose have a -200 suffix after their designation, this deriving from the serial number range of the first French aircraft thus equipped.

Below:
With the exception of built-in 30mm DEFA cannon, the Mirage F1B trainer has the same combat potential as its single-seat companion.

Mirage F1 weapon load options.

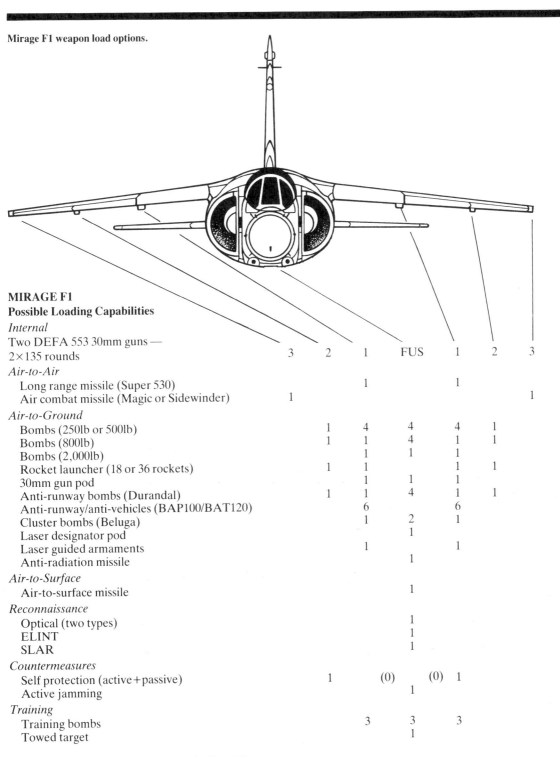

MIRAGE F1
Possible Loading Capabilities

	3	2	1	FUS	1	2	3
Internal							
Two DEFA 553 30mm guns — 2×135 rounds							
Air-to-Air							
Long range missile (Super 530)			1		1		
Air combat missile (Magic or Sidewinder)	1						1
Air-to-Ground							
Bombs (250lb or 500lb)		1	4	4	4	1	
Bombs (800lb)		1	1	4	1	1	
Bombs (2,000lb)			1	1	1		
Rocket launcher (18 or 36 rockets)		1	1		1	1	
30mm gun pod			1	1	1		
Anti-runway bombs (Durandal)		1	1	4	1	1	
Anti-runway/anti-vehicles (BAP100/BAT120)			6		6		
Cluster bombs (Beluga)			1	2	1		
Laser designator pod				1			
Laser guided armaments			1		1		
Anti-radiation missile				1			
Air-to-Surface							
Air-to-surface missile				1			
Reconnaissance							
Optical (two types)				1			
ELINT				1			
SLAR				1			
Countermeasures							
Self protection (active+passive)		1	(0)		(0)	1	
Active jamming				1			
Training							
Training bombs			3	3	3		
Towed target				1			

(0) Wing station ZERO specific for chaff and flares

Ease of support (which means quick reaction and more sorties flown in wartime) was a high priority for Dassault in designing the Mirage F1 and its weapon systems. A low landing speed (232km/hr or 144mph in current models) enables the aircraft to operate from short airfields, whilst turn-round time is claimed to be 15min between two interception missions, including 6min for a full replacement of internal fuel via a pressure system. Ground handling equipment can be moved by air, although maintenance requirements are said to be commendably low at 4.5 hours per flying hour. A typical major job would be three hours for four men to change the engine — currently a 7,200kg (15,870lb) thrust ATAR 9K-50. To maintain the aircraft at a high state of in-cockpit readiness, cutting reaction time to 2min, the GAMO alert unit is available in the form of a vehicle which supplies electrical power for pre-heating systems, radar cooling and cockpit air conditioning via an umbilical cord (and even includes a parasol on a telescopic arm to shade the pilot!). Selection of the engine-starting procedure automatically withdraws the GAMO unit, and the aircraft is ready to go. The complete navigation and weapons system can be checked and any faults identified in under 15min by the SDAP automated maintenance system contained in an air-portable trailer.

External weapons weighing up to 6,300kg (13,900lb) can be carried by the Mirage F1 on three Alkan universal stores carriers, two outboard underwing pylons, and the wing tips (MATRA 550 Magic or AIM-9 Sidewinder AAMs). For interception, a MATRA Super 530 AAM usually occupies each inboard wing pylon, having the ability to destroy a target whose altitude may be up to 30,000ft (9,150m) above or below the Mirage. For surface attack the weapon possibilities are extensive, starting with up to 14 250kg (552lb) bombs, or 144 Thomson-Brandt rockets. Missiles such as the MATRA ARMAT anti-radar weapon and Aérospatiale AM-39 Exocet are potential loads, as is the Aérospatiale AS-30L with its associated laser designator pod on the centreline pylon. ECM pods, often the MATRA Sycomor, are also used by some Mirage F1 customers, the first of which was — of course — the Armée de l'Air.

French requirements for the Mirage F1 were initially restricted to the all-weather interceptor role, where ageing Vautour IINs were due for retirement, followed by Super Mystère B2s and, ultimately, Mirage IIICs. For this reason orders were placed only for the F1C ('C' indicating 'Chasseur', or pursuit) version — the first, in 1969, covering 30 aircraft. Batches of 55 and 20 were funded in 1971 and 1973 to complete the first-stage target of 105 to be delivered by June 1977. Eleven more fighters were added in 1976, whilst the 1977-82 defence plan was to account for a further 109, making 225 in all. An unprogrammed 21 were added in 1981, for a total of 246, despite which official statements insisted in counting the six prototypes (including two F1CRs) to make 252 all told. As an economy measure, the last 21 were cancelled in 1982 and not replaced, leaving the recce contract short. As shown in the table, France will get four F1 fighter prototypes, 164 fighter versions (81 F1Cs and 83 F1C-200s), 20 F1Bs and 43 F1CRs (two of the last-mentioned being recce prototypes).

	F1B	F1C/-200	F1CR
Prototypes—		4	2
1969	—	30	—
1971	—	55	—
1973	—	20	—
1976	—	11	—
1977	6	24	—
1978	9	24	—
1979	5	—	18
1980	—	—	23
Totals	20	168	43

Wearing a large number '1' on its nose, the first production F1C was flown at Bordeaux by Guy Mitaux-Maurouard on 15 February 1973 — a few months later than planned. Delivered to the CEV in March, it was subsequently joined at Istres by No 5. Service trials by the CEAM at Mont-de-Marsan were handled by Nos 2, 3 and 4 which were delivered from 14 May onwards and wore the codes 118-AK, 118-AL and 118-AM respectively (continuing to do so at the time of writing, serving with EC 24/118, the CEAM component operated by CAFDA — Air Defence Command — for ongoing trials).

It was to Mont-de-Marsan that personnel of the premier French all-weather interceptor wing, EC 30, were posted to convert to the new aircraft. First to arrive were some 100 technicians in August 1973, followed by a dozen pilots in September, and after the ground school phase, the latter began flying in October. Transition rapidly accomplished, the first seven aircraft and pilots returned to their operational base at Reims-Champagne on 20 December, joining the 'Normandie-Niemen' squadron: Escadron de Chasse Tous Temps 2/30. The Mirage F1s already wore their squadron markings on arrival, the first being No 6, coded 30-MA. ('Niemen' will not be found on any maps of France, for the second part of the Normandy squadron's name stems from its

Above:
ECTT 30 at Reims-Champagne was the first wing to re-equip with Mirage F1Cs. The wing's two squadrons are represented here by '30-MP' of ECTT 2/30 'Normandie-Niemen' and '30-FA' from ECTT 3/30 'Lorraine'.

operation alongside the Red Air Force in World War 2 and a battle honour awarded by Stalin for the Niemen offensive. Ties with former allies were renewed on 24 July 1977 when six Mirage F1Cs flew to Kubinka, 80km/50 miles south of Moscow, on a five-day courtesy visit.)

ECTT 2/30 was soon up to strength with 18 pilots and 16 aircraft (Nos 6-21, including the wing's spare), and deliveries switched to its companion at Reims, ECTT 3/30 'Lorraine', which accepted Nos 23-37 (15 aircraft) and coded them straight through from 30-FA to 30-FO. The wing was officially declared to have completed its re-equipment on 5 July 1974 and had flown 13,000 hours by the end of 1975. Dassault had delivered 30 F1s by the end of April from a production rate of one per week.

At first, pilots selected to fly the F1C were required to have a minimum of 700 flying hours to their credit, whether they were ex-Vautours or had been posted from other squadrons because of prior experience with single-seat combat aircraft. Their conversion usually comprised between 11 and 14 handling flights and 25 operational evaluation sorties — all on the F1C, as the two-seat F1B was only on the drawing board. Later, however, the restrictions were relaxed and junior pilots began arriving straight from flying school.

In parallel with its training duties, ECTT 30 was charged with preparing a report on the Mirage F1 in squadron service, and this was generally favourable despite the newness of the aircraft. The cockpit was assessed to be comfortable and well-planned, with a clear and rational layout of instruments and controls. Noise level and air conditioning were rated excellent. Flight controls received praise for smoothness at all speeds, and in its production form the Mirage F1 was found to have an approach speed of 352km/hr (219mph) and a touchdown speed in the region of 250-260km/hr (155-162mph). Approach and touch-down angles of incidence were much reduced and the landing run was 800m (2,625ft), or 600m (1,970ft) when the braking parachute was used. In examining the Atar 9K50 engine, pilots reported that it has a practically instantaneous throttle response, and afterburner can be used over a wide range of manoeuvres. Furthermore, the throttle can be moved from idle to full power, even with afterburner operative, in one single movement, without intermediate positions. A useful attribute in air combat is that the compressor will not stall at very high altitude, thus permitting full power to be selected when needed.

The F1 possesses an integrated navigation system — the first in a French aircraft to combine an autopilot, VOR-ILS and TACAN — and crews were pleased to note that the autopilot could be switched in at any stage of the flight and used for fully-automatic approaches. With an internal fuel load of 4,200litres (924gal), the Mirage F1C has a range of 1,100km (685 miles), so that a typical mission could involve: take-off, climb, 10min holding at altitude, acceleration from Mach 2.0 to 2.2, and attack. Sufficient fuel remains available at 50,000ft after acceleration to Mach 2.0 for a pursuit phase of 8min. Cyrano IV radar automatically locks on to and tracks a target to permit blind firing and can be used with range displays of 110, 65 and 28km (68, 40 and 17 miles). An X-band pulse radar, Cyrano IV is adapted for air-to-air and air-to-ground operation, though the better ground picture given by its short wave-length is offset by poor air interception performance in bad weather.

Of crucial importance in air fighting is the pilot's field of vision which, thanks to a downwards-tilted nose and larger front panels, is between 5° and 12° more than the NATO requirement. Aft view is 60°, whilst the pilot can see over 50° downwards. The Mirage F1's thin wing gives better trans-sonic performance than the Mirage III, and the combination of higher aspect ratio and taper ratio provide improved steady turn capability. A high wing and low tailplane mean that high-g manoeuvres can be undertaken throughout the flight envelope without the risk of deep stall. The F1 will turn at 21°/sec, whilst at medium altitude it is able to maintain a steady turn between 500km/hr (311mph) indicated airspeed and Mach 0.95. Over 7g can be pulled at Mach 2.2, or over 8g at subsonic speeds.

The two squadrons of Mirage IIICs of EC 5 at Orange-Caritat were the next to give way to the F1C, and EC 1/5 'Vendée' received its first in mid-1974, coding them from 5-NA onwards. EC 2/5 'Ile de France' (5-OA and up) had completed re-requipment of the wing, as it then stood, by mid-1975. The 80th F1 of all types was delivered in May 1975 and the 56th for French use that August. On 17 July 1975 the Mirage F1 clocked-up its 10,000th service hour without loss, and the 50,000 point was passed late in 1977. At that time serviceability had increased to 85%, having been 34.6% in 1974, 45% in 1975, 48% in 1976 and 59% during the first half of 1977. Late in 1979 100,000 hours was attained — 45,000 contributed by ECTT 30, 33,000 by EC 5 and 22,000 by EC 12.

Training support for later units was the responsibility of ECTT 30, so that between February and September 1976 personnel of the 'Cornouailles' squadron of EC 12, operator of Dassault Super Mystère B2s at Cambrai-Epinoy, were posted to Reims for conversion. 'Cornouailles', at that time designated EC 2/12, was equipped with Mirage F1Cs beginning No 79 (12-ZA), this aircraft being the first fitted with an RWR (radar warning receiver) installation in the form of small bullet-shaped fairings on the fin leading and trailing edges. The squadron achieved its initial operating capability with eight F1Cs on 1 October 1976. EC 1/12 'Cambresis' began transition to second-hand aircraft when it took delivery of No 13 on 31 January 1977, this F1C adopting the code 12-YA. The process was completed when the last Super Mystères were withdrawn on 9 September 1977.

All 105 aircraft in the first three batches had been delivered by the end of 1978, but only 83 wore French markings, the last of which was numbered 103. Of the remainder, 16 were transferred at random to expedite a Greek contract, four were retained by Dassault for modifications, and Nos 104-105 were switched to a new contract. The new aircraft in question was the Mirage F1C-200, a variant clearly identified by the fixed in-flight refuelling probe mounted at the base of the pilot's windscreen on the starboard side. F1C-200s began a fresh serialling range at No 201, this particular aircraft being a conversion of the first production F1C, No 1. In all there were 24 probed aircraft in the initial batch (including two refurbished F1Cs and four which had been held back) which, added to the remaining 81 non-IFR

aircraft, completed the first series of contracts for 105. Previously it had been proposed that 35 of the 105 would be modified. Further production continued from No 225, and ended at No 283 in 1983.

Though produced for export, Mirage F1B trainers did not enter AA service until early 1981 when the first of 20 was delivered to the CEAM, their serials beginning at No 501. Availability of extra fighters allowed formation of additional squadrons, though the first 24 Srs 200s went to EC 1/5 and 2/5 to replace earlier models. Uniquely, these two units are entirely equipped with -200s because of their rapid overseas intervention role, the others having a mixture of both variants. EC 5 received F1C-200 No 202 for evaluation early in 1977, followed by main

Below:
Third of the home Mirage F1C wings was EC 12 at Cambrai-Epinoy. The attractive fin art has since been reduced in size by official order.

Above:
The first 'production' Mirage F1C-200, No 201, was a rebuild of No 1 — as betrayed by the absence of bullet-shaped radar warning receiver antennae on the fin leading and trailing edges. No 201 is assigned to the CEAM for development work.

Below:
Taxying at Creil-Senlis, a Mirage F1C of EC 1/10 'Valois'. The squadron joined ECTT 30 at Reims in 1985.

deliveries from early 1978, though the type's large-scale operational debut was not until 5 April 1981, when four made a non-stop flight from Solenzara, Corsica, to Djibouti as a demonstration of the rapid reinforcement capability. The probe can be installed or removed in about two hours and has little effect on performance up to Mach 1.4, top speed in this configuration being Mach 1.9.

The next squadron to form was a third component for the Cambrai Wing, EC 2/12 'Picardie' coming into being on 1 June 1980 with aircraft in the 12-KA code range, though at first most of its acquisitions were merely on loan from other units until further aircraft became available from the manufacturer. ('Cornouailles' — the old EC 2/12 — was renumbered EC 3/12 on 1 June 1979.) Two more units were established in 1981, of which EC 3/5 'Comtat Venaissin' was formed on 1 April with two-seat trainers at Orange. Three were on charge at a formal commissioning ceremony on 3 July 1981 when the wing also celebrated its 2,000th F1C-200 mid-air refuelling sortie and 50,000 hours on the Mirage F1. The F1B may be fitted with a dummy refuelling probe for training purposes and can carry a cannon pod to compensate for loss of internal armament.

Though the intended complement was 15 trainers, the OCU had received 19 F1Bs by 1983, these starting at No 501/5-AA and ending with No 520/5-AT. In addition, three F1C-200s are in use for single-seat instruction. The 'missing' F1B is the CEAM's No 502 '118-AT', for which the code 5-AB is being kept open in anticipation of this aircraft being eventually delivered. The gap has

Above:
**The second production Mirage F1B for the Armée de l'Air
is assigned to the CEAM. A dummy IFR probe can be
attached (à la F1C-200) for training purposes.**

been carefully left in order to preserve the
alpha-numerical code/serial sequence of the
trainers. Keeping codes and serials in such a tidy
form, though having great appeal to the military
mind, is more difficult when single-seat aircraft
from a much larger pool of reserves are involved,
and only EC 2/12 has attempted it — repainting
aircraft markings at frequent intervals as a result.

Starting in May 1981 EC 1/10 'Valois' worked-
up on Mirage F1Cs at Reims before returning to its
base at Creil-Senlis, there to join EC 2/10, for
whose Mirage IIICs there was to be no
replacement. Transfer of Creil to a care and
maintenance basis resulted in 'Valois' joining the
Reims wing, in preparation for which it had
relinquished all its -200 series aircraft early in 1984.
At the end of 1981 only one of CAFDA's 10
home-based squadrons (EC 2/10) was not equipped with Mirage F1s, the position having changed
in July 1983 when EC 2 at Dijon joined the
Command prior to trading in its Mirage IIIEs for
2000Cs.

Initially the F1C was limited in its armament to
just the two internal DEFA 553 cannon, pending
arrival of its two new missiles. This certainly
allowed pilots full opportunity to practice their
gunnery during the 180 or so hours they flew in the
course of about 200 sorties per year, and by 1976
firing scores were 52%. The 135 rounds for each
gun are sufficient for just seven seconds, though
this may be doubled by using one weapon at a
time. Some 70% of training was allocated to
air-to-air practice and the remainder to ground
attack, also with bombs and rockets, including
10-15% night flying. After service trials at CEV
Cazaux in December 1976, and evaluation by EC 5
during the following year, the infra-red homing
MATRA 550 Magic AAM was issued to units in
1978 and installed at the wingtip, followed by the
semi-active radar homing MATRA Super 530F-1,

officially issued to EC 12 in December 1979 (first
rounds having been handed-over in September
1978). Whereas the Magic is a close-range or
dogfight weapon with a minimum range of 300m
(985ft), the Super 530F-1 is a long-distance,
all-weather AAM effective up to 80,000ft and
against aircraft which may be 25,000ft above or
below the interceptor. First double launch trials of
the Super 530 took place from a Mirage F1C on
7 November 1983.

There is provision on the F1C for a Super 530
beneath the fuselage and one on each inner wing
pylon, as an alternative to fuel tanks, the outer
strongpoints normally remaining unused in the air
defence role. One or more of the Super 530s may
be replaced by a first-generation MATRA 530FE,
which has about half the range of its 'Super'
derivative, and may be readily recognised by
traditionally-shaped (pointed) fins and an infra-red
seeker nose. This variant had its service trials at
Cazaux between 7 and 18 December 1977 when
about 15 were launched by Mirage F1Cs from EC 5
and EC 30. The primary role of EC 5 is low-level
interception with both the 530FE and Magic,
whilst ECTT 30 is assigned to high-level, high-
speed missions with 530FEs (first carried underwing in February 1976). EC 12, as noted, is able to
cover the intermediate heights with its Super 530s.

Mirage F1C-200s were deployed to Africa in
1983 when Libyan-backed guerillas launched an
invasion of Chad, a former French colony which
retains contacts with Paris. After pre-positioning
in Gabon and the Central African Republic, four
AA Mirage F1s and four Jaguars took up station at
N'Djamena, the capital of Chad, on 21 August,
the former to provide air defence for the airlifting

of some 3,000 French troops. The operation was successful in promoting an uneasy cease-fire, and though Jaguars were involved in some ground-attack missions, the Mirages' lives were less eventful.

Meanwhile, the Armée de l'Air was introducing its final F1 variant to operational service: the F1CR. Stemming from a requirement to replace the Mirage IIIR and IIIRD with ER 33, the F1CR was flown at Istres in prototype form by Dassault pilot M. Fremond on 20 November 1981, having been converted from a standard F1C-200 taken off the production line. A second aircraft soon joined the programme, the pair initially flying with the numbers 01 and 02 until they were changed to 601 and 602 late in 1982 — when the number of F1CRs officially on order suddenly increased from 62 to 64. Both were retained for company trials, whilst the first production aircraft (No 603) went to the CEAM as 118-AA soon after its initial flight on 10 November 1982. All recce aircraft are known as F1CRs despite the fact that they carry a refuelling probe and therefore qualify for a -200 suffix.

As usual, pilots were trained at CEAM between April and June 1983 before ER 33 took delivery of its first F1CR at Strasbourg-Entzheim on 1 July, ER 2/33 'Savoie' officially placing the type in service on 7 September. At this time, seven of the planned 15 had been received and 15 of 18 pilots trained, the aircraft using codes in the range beginning 33-NA. Hopes had previously been expressed that the AA would have four squadrons of F1CRs, but the cancellation of 21 aircraft has made it unlikely that ER 33's three units will be completely re-equipped except, perhaps, by F1Cs carrying only external sensors in a pod beneath the centreline. 'Savoie' was complete by December 1983, after which ER 1/33 'Belfort' began training. The squadron whose future is in doubt is ER 3/33 'Moselle', presently with Mirage IIIRDs.

Although two of ER 33's three squadrons are assigned a secondary ground-attack role, all

Above:

Additional attack duties assigned to the first Mirage F1CR-200 reconnaissance squadron — ER 2/33 'Savoie' — are revealed by underwing MATRA F4 pods containing 18 68mm rockets.

F1CRs can be equipped with Magic AAMs on the wingtips for self defence. From August 1984 each F1CR squadron is being equipped with a MATRA SARA tactical recce ground station — air transportable by Transall C-160 — comprising between seven and nine cabins containing flight-planning facilities, operational and command communications, interpretation apparatus and equipment for receiving data transmissions from F1CRs still in flight. For training purposes another Dassault aircraft, Falcon 20 No 451, has been specially fitted with the F1CR's avionics system in the left-hand seat, together with a fighter-type control stick. It made its initial flight in this configuration on 4 May 1984.

Many more years remain for the Mirage F1 in French service, though not all of this will be in the air defence role. As the Mirage 2000C comes to the fore, so the F1 is expected to transfer to the still important task of ground attack. Naturally, it will carry the range of bombs, rockets and self-defence aids already in use with Mirage IIIE units, but a new addition to the armoury will be the Aérospatiale AS 30L ASM. Based on the earlier AS 30, but fitted with a laser seeker head, the 'L' version undertook service trials in 1984 before first issues were made to Jaguar squadrons. It will later be applied to the F1C for precision strikes against surface targets, guided by any standard NATO laser — whether aimed by the carrier aircraft, a companion or a forward air controller on the ground. Already, however, the Mirage F1 is well-versed in air-to-surface operations, for overseas customers have bought over 400, together with armament appropriate to their particular needs.

In common with its delta predecessor, the Mirage F1 has found a ready market outside France, its export customers comprising some previous operators of Mirage IIIs and others shopping with Dassault for the first time. They also nearly included a sizeable portion of NATO following a hard fight against American competition in what came to be known as the 'Sale of the Century'. Though other export customers had been secured well before Dassault took on the combined forces of General Dynamics and Northrop, discussion of their contracts will be deferred until after mention has been made of the aircraft which almost became Western Europe's prime fighter: the Mirage F1 International.

During the early 1970s Belgium, Denmark, the Netherlands and Norway began seriously to look for a multi-role aircraft to replace their Lockheed Starfighters, preferably from local production programmes. Between them these four countries would require an initial 350 aircraft, with the strong possibility (since confirmed) of follow-on orders totalling another 200 or so. The US industry fiercely promoted the Northrop YF-17 Cobra (perhaps now better known in its developed form as the McDonnell Douglas F/A-18 Hornet) and General Dynamics's YF-16 (Fighting Falcon), while the European front-runner was a new Mirage F1 variant. The key aspect of the home aircraft was its new SNECMA M53 Super Atar engine which, rated at 8,500kg (18,740lb) thrust with reheat, was considerably more powerful than the Atar 9K50. Thus powered, the newcomer was alternatively known as the F1E or F1 M53.

For the French aviation industry the M53 was an important — though short-step forward. The Atar, designed in 1946 around an older German design,

was a thoroughly reliable 'bird in the hand' engine ideally suited to Mirage customers not wishing to take the risk of buying a 'two in the bush' new powerplant which might or might not live up to the promises in its maker's brochure. In the M53 SNECMA sought to develop a new generation engine with 'experience' already built in, and so it opted for the bypass turbojet rather than going the whole way to the fuel-efficient turbofan which was then establishing itself as a power source for military aircraft. As an 'almost turbofan' the M53 would satisfy the cautious customer; though a new engine in France, it contained little with which other Western nations had not been familiar for a decade. (Earlier work on the troublesome TF104, TF106 and TF306 advanced turbofans in association with Pratt & Whitney, probably convinced SNECMA that simplicity should be its watchword in the next venture.)

A private venture for two years previously, the F1 M53 got off the ground in a figurative sense on 16 March 1973 when the French government gave its blessing to a programme 'to promote close international co-operation between the French aerospace industry and the aerospace industries of other countries, in particular European countries, which, in the event of a successful outcome, will lead to long-lasting alliances.' This statement went some way towards assuring potential customers that the F1 M53 was more than a paper aeroplane, and it was later backed by a declaration that the

Below:
More sophisticated avionics and a SNECMA M53 engine characterised the original Mirage F1E multi-role aircraft. Begun as a private venture, the variant was adopted officially as France's bid to produce a new NATO fighter.

Armée de l'Air would have at least 40, and probably up to 120, if at least two others placed orders. This was news to the AA, which had no requirement for an F1E and had on several occasions stated its lack of interest in an aircraft costing about 20% more than its F1Cs.

Also intended to power the twin-engined Dassault ACF advanced combat aircraft, the M53 began its bench testing in February 1970, though it did not take to the air until July 1973, in the starboard pod of a Caravelle testbed. Two months later, the F1 M53 mock-up was completed at St Cloud and work was under way on the prototype, this to be followed by a demonstrator and a two-seat F1D trainer. Orders were also placed for 20 engines, comprising three for bench testing, a development batch of 10 to be used for air and ground trials, three for supersonic flight in the F1, and four for the ACF which were scheduled to fly in July 1976.

Guy Mitaux-Maurouard took the first F1E into the air at Istres on 22 December 1974, achieving Mach 1.35 and 38,000ft in the course of a sortie lasting one hour. Making rapid progress immediately prior to the festive season, the F1 M53 gained Mach 1.65 on its second flight and Mach 1.84 on the fourth (both 23 December), and on Christmas Eve Maurouard reached Mach 2.05. Little time was lost in showing the prospective international fighter to representatives of the four possible purchasers, these examining the aircraft on

8 January following its sixth and seventh sorties on the previous two days. After completing a series of 19 flights totalling 20 hours, the aircraft was stood-down for maintenance and did not fly again until 21 March.

Shorter than the Atar 9K50, the M53 required a little modification of the Mirage F1, including a fuselage 23mm longer, slightly larger air intakes for a mass flow increased from 72 to 84kg/sec (158 to 185lb/sec) and a rear fuselage marginally larger. In terms of avionics, the F1E was to be better equipped than its predecessor, especially with regard to an inertial navigation system, head-up display and the improved Cyrano IV-100 radar. Performance was greatly improved, the list of achievements including 4,000ft (1,200m) on the ceiling, an extra 12,000ft/min (60m/sec) initial climb rate and no less than twice that at 34,000ft, a further +0.7g on the steady turn rate at Mach 0.95, 2.5min off the time to 40,000ft and 105km (65 miles) on the hi-lo-hi range with four 1,000lb (454kg) bombs. But the Europeans were not impressed.

Four export versions of the aircraft had been prepared to interest the main NATO prospects: F1EB for Belgium; F1ED for Denmark; F1EN for the Netherlands; and F1FV for Norway. Unquestionably these had a performance which would please any air force; what they lacked was high technology to keep sub-contractors satisfied and provide room for further 'growth' — eg, an advanced engine, fly-by-wire controls and an airframe including composite structures. No amount of obfuscation by Dassault could disguise that fact, though as the competition neared its climax, claims and counter claims, allegations and counter allegations passed between the participants. Typical of these was an assertion that the M53 was cleared for Mach 2.5 — made after the Assemblée Nationale had been told that the F1E could not exceed Mach 2.2 without changes to the cockpit and wing leading edges. The blow came on 7 June 1975, when the GD F-16 was announced winner of the 'Sale of the Century'. Adding salt to the wound, the decision was revealed at the Paris Salon.

The F1E abruptly vanished from the show, only to return a couple of days later in a patriotic red, white and blue colour scheme. This was a last, defiant gesture, though a scapegoat for the humiliation was quickly found when it was revealed that a former Chief of Air Staff had been a consultant to Northrop (the other loser) during the competition. Whilst the 'Paul Stehlin Affair' was running its course and France was castigating its NATO neighbours for being un-European (conveniently forgetting, of course, that at least *they* had not walked out of the Alliance at a moment's notice), the air force quietly dropped the F1E. No further aircraft of the type were produced, and the prototype was grounded for almost 18 months before beginning a series of M53 engine trials for the Mirage 2000. Designations F1 M53 and F1E became no longer interchangeable, the former also vanishing from the scene, whilst the latter reverted to its function of describing a Mirage F1 with multi-role avionics.

Undoubtedly Dassault had lost a major sale, but for the very reasons of simplicity and reliability · which made the Mirage F1 the natural choice of many other air forces. In addition to the home country, 10 have now bought F1s, brief details of which will be found hereunder.

Ecuador   In 1977 the US government thwarted Ecuadorean plans to purchase 24 IAI Kfirs by exercising its right of veto on exports of that aircraft's General Electric J79 engine. Instead, the

Fuerza Aérea Ecuatoriana began negotiations with Dassault apparently for replacement Mirage IIIs or 5s, but in the event an order for 16 Mirage F1JA radar-equipped aircraft and two F1JE trainers was announced later the same year. Deliveries began to 2110° Escuadron de Combate at Taura air base in January 1979 and were completed in the middle of the following year with the two trainers, although one F1JA was lost in an accident on 25 June 1980.

Greece   During the early 1970s Greece formulated a requirement for replacement of its Convair F-102 interceptors but was unable to obtain US combat aircraft (which would almost certainly have been Phantoms) because of American disapproval of the military government in Athens. Instead, 40 Mirage F1CGs and a supply of MATRA 550 Magic AAMs were ordered from France as a matter of urgency, and to expedite their delivery to the Elliniki Aeroporia, the first 16 were diverted from production for the Armée de l'Air, beginning with what would have been No 51. None had the fin-mounted RWR bullet fairings.

The first aircraft was handed over in France on 29 January 1975, and two were lost during training before deliveries began to Greece on 5 August 1975. The final F1CG arrived two years later and all were issued to 114a Pterix Mahis (Combat Wing) at Tanagra, northwest of Athens, to be operated by 334 'Thalos' and 342 'Sparta' Mire Anagaitiseos (Interceptor Squadrons). Tanagra is also the base of the Hellenic Aerospace Industry, which has operated a Mirage F1 overhaul facility

Below:
Ecuador received 16 Mirage F1JAs in 1979-80, their camouflage colours being two shades of green.

Top:
Forty Mirage F1CGs were supplied to Greece for two all-weather interceptor squadrons. The final delivery, shown here, was in 1977.

Above:
The Gulf war has resulted in accelerated deliveries of Mirages to Iraq. The second of the three batches to be delivered, in 1983, was of Mirage F1EQ-200s.

since 1981 and may take on the care of F1s operated by some Arab countries. In April 1984 France offered Greece 20 more Mirage F1s as interim equipment in the hope of swinging the next major fighter buy in favour of Mirage 2000s, instead of US aircraft. The gesture was declined, Greece apparently having a poor opinion of French after-sales service. At the time, it was noted that only 30 F1CGs remain in service.

Iraq Following the issue of large arms contracts to the Soviet Union, Iraq turned to the West late in 1976 and placed an order in June of the following year for an initial 36 Mirage F1s, with options on a

further number, plus a large quantity of MATRA 550 Magic AAMs. Late in 1979 24 of these options were taken up, whilst another 29 were added to the requirement in 1982. Shortly before deliveries were about to begin, and whilst pilots were receiving training at Mont-de-Marsan, Iraq launched an invasion of Iran in September 1980. Resisting diplomatic pressure not to supply war material, France allowed deliveries to go ahead and the first four Mirages passed through Larnaca, Cyprus on 31 January 1981, supposedly on delivery to Jordan. This batch comprised 30 multi-role F1EQs and six F1BQ trainers, of which all had been completed by mid-1981.

Though a French spokesman said in January 1981 that it would be 'another five years' before the other two batches were delivered to al Quwwat al Jawwiya al Iraqiya, further aircraft began appearing early in 1983. These were seen to be fitted with flight-refuelling probes in the usual position, and are believed to comprise 23 F1EQ-200s and six F1BQs. (The designation of the two-seaters is uncertain, as their FR probes may only be dummies for training purposes.) The final

24 aircraft (which seem to constitute the second order) are equipped to fire Aérospatiale AM39 Exocet anti-ship missiles, for which reason they have Agave radar in the nose. Also fitted with flight-refuelling probes, they comprise at least two trainers plus F1EQ5-200 single-seat variants, delivery to Iraq having begun with the first eight in October 1984. They have been involved in some of the Exocet attacks against oil tankers in the Arabian Gulf, the first successful mission being in late-February 1985 following an initial failed attempt (due to missile interface problems) the previous 3 December.

Jordan The Royal Jordan Air Force — al Quwwat al Jawwiya al Malakiya al Urduniya — received Saudi Arabian finance for a Mirage F1 purchase in mid-1979 after the US goverment refused Amman permission to buy F-16 fighting Falcons to replace ageing F-104A Starfighters. The first batch of aircraft contained 17 F1CJ interceptors and two F1BJ trainers, on which training was undertaken in France during the early months of 1981. Operated by No 25 Squadron at Mwaffaq Salti, near Azraq, the 16 remaining F1Cs are armed with both MATRA 530 and 550 Magic AAMs. An option was meanwhile taken-up for 17 multi-role F1EJs and these were supplied to No 25 Squadron, also at Mwffaq Salti, during the first half of 1983. In September 1984 it was revealed that Jordan would be receiving a further 10 Mirage F1s — although according to the wording of the statement, only 33 Mirages had been delivered by that time, and would be joined by an additional 13. The 10 appeared to have been ordered in 1983.

Kuwait In 1974, a year after there had been border clashes with Iraqi forces, Kuwait placed an order for 18 Mirage F1CK interceptors and two F1BK trainers to supersede the BAC Lightnings which it found too complex to operate efficiently. Simultaneous armament contracts covered MATRA Super 530s and 550 Magics. F1CKs were handed over for training to begin in France during March 1976, and first deliveries were made that July. The last followed just a year later, though one was destroyed in an accident before leaving France. The two trainers ordered by Kuwait were the first of the type, a prototype of which was flown on 26 May 1976, reaching Mach 1.51 at 37,000ft in the course of its maiden one-hour sortie. This and the second aircraft were delivered on 26 October and 4 November 1977 to complete the contract.

During 1982 there were reports that Kuwait planned to buy Mirage 2000s, but these were denied in January 1983 by the air force C-in-C, who revealed that 12 more Mirage F1s had been ordered, together with MATRA Super 530 AAMs. There are suggestions that the French arms contract placed by Kuwait in May 1983 contained MATRA ARMAT anti-radiation missiles (developed from the Anglo-French MARTEL ASM) for the F1s. Priority deliveries of the 12 aircraft — in conjunction with an attrition-replacement trainer — were due to have been completed by mid-1985, probably to be based with the original aircraft at Ali Salim Sabah.

Libya A previous Mirage 5 customer, al Quwwat al Jawwiya al Libiyya, ordered 38 Mirage F1s in 1974, delivery of which began three years later. These were 16 F1AD ground attack versions (at least some of which, unusually, have flight-refuell-

Below:
A rare picture of an Iraqi Mirage F1B fitted with an IFR probe.

Pictured during a lively demonstration of low-altitude manoeuvrability at the 1983 International Air Tattoo is a Mirage F1EJ of the Royal Jordanian Air Force.

ing probes), 16 multi-role F1EDs with Super 530 and Magic AAMs, and six F1BD trainers. They are operated by two squadrons based at Okba Ben Nafi — the former Wheelus USAF base. Though the F1EDs were supposedly serialled 501-516, further aircraft marked 527-541 have been reported — possibly the result of a re-allocation of markings.

Morocco As part of an extensive air defence system finally completed in mid-1981, al Quwwat al Jawwiya al Malakiya Marakishiya ordered 25 Mirage F1CH interceptors late in 1975 together with MATRA 530 and Magic AAMs. Options were held on a further 50, of which 25 were taken up in 1977 and delivered as multi-role F1EHs from 1978 onwards. All had been completed by mid-1980, though most of the final nine seem to have spent the next two years at Bordeaux — a fact

Below:
No 25 Squadron of the RJAF flies Mirage F1CJs in the air superiority role. Aircraft are finished in light blue, this one carrying RP35 drop-tanks of 1,200litre (264gal) capacity.

possibly not unconnected with the serious financial problems being suffered by Morocco at that time. Based at Agadir and Marrakech, plus detachments, the Mirages have been used operationally against Polisario guerilla forces in the annexed territory of Western Sahara. Several have been lost on such missions, two of them shot down by SAMs on 13 October 1981, and another on 14 January 1985.

Qatar Previously operating nothing more potent than four Hawker Hunters, Qatar ordered 12 Mirage F1EDAs and a pair of F1DDA trainers late in 1979. When the aircraft failed to appear a couple of years later there was speculation that the contract had been cancelled, but it was not until four years after the order that the first single and two-seat F1s began pilot training at Orange, France. They were delivered in mid-1984.

South Africa A contract for an undisclosed number of Mirage F1s was placed by the Suid Afrikaanse Lugmag and as a hedge against a political embargo the Armaments Development & Production Corporation secured a manufacturing licence for both airframe and engine, though this has yet to be exercised apart from the manufacture of some spare parts. The aircraft emerged as 16 F1CZ interceptors and 32 ground-attack F1AZs, first examples of both appearing anonymously at the 1975 Paris Air Show, shortly before delivery.

The F1CZs were supplied to No 3 Squadron at Waterkloof and armed with MATRA 530 and 550 Magic AAMS, though indigenous Armscor V-3 Kukri has supplemented the latter — with which it shares a strong external similarity. Two interceptors were lost in a collision in February 1979 and are reported to have been replaced by aircraft wearing the same serial numbers (203 and 204).

No 1 Squadron, at Hoedspruit, received all 32 F1AZs. Both units were part of Strike Command when formed, but in January 1980 they were included in the newly-established Air Defence Command (Lugruimbeheerkommandemente) which has its HQ at Silvermijn.

Spain Expanding its fighter force, including Mirage IIIs, the Ejército del Aire placed an initial order for 15 Mirage F1CEs which received the local designation C.14, later C.14A, and were delivered to Escuadrón 141 of Ala de Caza 14 (14th Fighter Wing) at Los Llanos/Albacete from May 1975 onwards. Nine more were ordered in

Above:
Kuwait received Mirage F1 trainers even before the French Air Force, this being the first F1BK.

Below:
Two Mirage F1DDA trainers were delivered to Qatar in 1984, accompanied by 12 F1EDAs.

Top:
No 3 Squadron of the SAAF flies Mirage F1CZ interceptors from Hoedspruit.

Centre:
For attack operations the SAAF took delivery of 32 Mirage F1AZs, identifiable by their 'solid' noses. All are flown from Hoedspruit by No 1 Squadron.

Above:
Spain's Three Mirage F1 squadrons are each allocated one or two trainers. Included in the complement of Escuadrón 141 is this Mirage F1BE.

January 1977 and supplied from June 1978, whilst later contracts covered a single attrition replacement and, in 1978, a final batch of 48: six F1BE (CE.14A) trainers, 20 F1CEs and 22 F1EE-200 (CE.14B) multi-role aircraft. Ala 14

formed a second squadron, Esc 142, on 1 April 1980 when trainer deliveries began. Both units have a nominal establishment of 22 single-seat and two trainer aircraft and are assigned to Mando Aéreo de Combate (Air Combat Command).

A separate branch of the air force, Mando Aéreo de Canarias, is responsible for defence of the Canary Islands, where remoteness requires interceptor and attack capabilities to be combined in one aircraft type for economy. Escuadrón 462 formed on 14 January 1982 as a Mirage F1EE unit, its first aircraft having been completed some nine months before. Deliveries ended in mid-1982, the 68th also being the 500th production Mirage F1 built, in April 1982. At this time France had received 167 F1s, including the two prototype recce aircraft, and production was running at seven per month.

4 The Mirage 2000

Return of the Delta

The complex method by which the Armée de l'Air acquired the Mirage F1 was not to be repeated in the case of the next Mirage to achieve production status, though the story of the Mirage 2000's adoption is only slightly less involved. Briefly, it began with French plans to develop an equivalent to the Panavia MRCA (Tornado) from the basis of the Mirage G8, the resultant aircraft — known as the G8A or F8 — having fixed-geometry wings swept at 55° and one or two seats according to role. Power was to be provided by two new SNECMA M53s. It was hardly surprising that Dassault called this the 'Super Mirage', whilst the air force knew the programme as the Avion de Combat Futur: ACF.

It was to be an expensive aircraft, costing FF50million per copy (at 1973 prices), when a Mirage F1 could be obtained for FF21million. Nothing daunted, the government pressed ahead with the programme and even ordered a second prototype in 1975, affirming a commitment to the ACF when others were questioning its viability. That the doubters might be justified seemed more likely in September of the same year when the second prototype was cancelled and funding for the project slowed down — this in spite of the fact that the M53 engine had received its production authorisation only a week before. The remaining ACF in the trials programme was due to fly in July 1976. Officials insisted in public that all which had changed was the rate at which the ACF was to progress, yet procurement targets had fallen from 200 to 100 because of high costs.

The ACF *was* too expensive, and when the National Defence Council met on 18 December 1975, under the chairmanship of President Giscard d'Estaing, it took the expected decision to cancel the aircraft. What was entirely unexpected — except by a few 'in the know' — was that a cheaper substitute had already been arranged. The very same meeting authorised a new programme called the Delta 2000 or Mirage 2000 which was to progress with all available speed to fill the gap. Having begun with a 1972 study called Delta 1000, the aircraft was quite well advanced when it suddenly came to the forefront, a home market for at least 200 already guaranteed.

Soon after the decision the air force Inspector-General, Gen Maurice Saint-Cricq, was questioned on the apparent about-face by the AA in adopting the simpler aircraft. Admitting that the Mirage 2000 did not meet the initial ambitions of the AA, he noted that these had proved less and less realistic over the past two years and could only have been achieved by giving the ACF virtual national priority. 'The Mirage 2000', he said, 'is thus a reasonable choice.' Clearly, the 2000 was a phoenix which had risen before the ACF's funeral pyre was properly alight, but its illegitimacy was soon rectified by the drafting of an operational requirement around its projected performance in March 1976. Some of the world's best aircraft have been private ventures in this vein, yet it does seem that France is making rather a habit of finding that it needs what Dassault produces, and not the other way about.

Plans were made to order 127 Mirage 2000s during the 1977-82 defence plan, these to include 10 production aircraft for delivery before the end of 1982. In a later statement on AA plans, Gen Saint-Cricq reiterated his opinion that the Mirage 2000 was a compromise, adding, however, that 'Nothing must be allowed to prevent this future combat aircraft from being ready for service by 1982'.

Having seen in earlier chapters that the delta layout was abandoned when Dassault acquired the ability to build the thinner wings of the Mirage F1, the reader may be led to assume that the Mirage 2000 was a retrograde step. Not so. Much had happened in the field of aerodynamics since the 1950s, and one of the great steps forward was the Control Configured Vehicle (CCV) concept, made possible by the application of a fly-by-wire (FBW) flight control system. This enabled the company to have the best of both worlds by retaining the delta's advantages whilst minimising its drawbacks.

Because of the shape a delta can have thick wings for fuel storage whilst maintaining a low thickness : chord ratio for high speed flight. It also has low drag, increased manoeuvrability, a smaller number of control surfaces (for extra reliability) and a decrease in radar detectability compared

Above:

The Mirage 2000 prototype exceeded Mach 1 during its maiden flight on 10 March 1978, piloted by Jean Coureau.

with a non-delta of otherwise similar type. This is offset to some extent by the need to deflect the trailing edge elevons for pitch control, thereby reducing the lift capability of the wing. In short, take-off and landing speeds are higher, longer runways required, and speed falls off during sharp turns. The block to progress was that a conventional aircraft has to have a fairly large static stability margin in all flying conditions to be properly flown, especially when the de-stabilising effects of external stores are taken into account. In a delta, with the C of G ahead of the wing's centre of pressure, equilibrium is maintained by moving the elevons upwards and causing downlift. With the CCV concept, involving a far smaller measure of artificial stability maintained by an onboard computer, the disadvantage is almost completely eliminated.

Like the abortive ACF, the Mirage 2000 was designed as a CCV with small canard-type foreplanes on the air intake trunks. It drew some of its technology from the variable stability Mirage IIIB which, between first flight on 17 February 1975 and 17 October the same year, had made 94 useful sorties at CEV, Istres, including the first fully-FBW flight on 8 September. New methods of construction were also investigated in a further

excursion into the realms of advanced technology. By mid-1976 a Mirage III had flown with a boron fibre rudder, and an F1 tested a complete stabilator of the same material throughout its flight envelope. With a weight saving of at least 15%, advantages were clear, so that the aircraft now has undercarriage doors, air brakes, canopy rear fairing, stabilators and most of the vertical fin of carbon or boron fibre. Some other equipment was also salvaged from the ACF, though much other earlier research had to be written off.

Priority within the priority programme was given to an air defence version of the 2000 for which Thomson-CSF and Électronique Marcel Dassault (now reflecting the name of the founder's son as Électronique Serge Dassault) were developing a pulse Doppler radar known as RDI (Radar Doppler à Impulsions), operating in the X-band — which has since been redesignated I/J-band. As a stand-by, Thomson-CSF continued work on the proven Cyrano, first as the Cyrano 500, then as the 100km (62-mile) range X-band RDM (Radar

Doppler Multifonction) — fortuitously, as it turned out. However, the medium-frequency repetition RDM, suitable for air-to-ground operation as well as air-to-air, is no second-best and is claimed to be at least equal to the Westinghouse system in the General Dynamics F-16 Fighting Falcon. Its flight-testing was begun in Vautour IIN No 337 in January 1980 and continued aboard Falcon 20 No 131 from June 1980 onwards. The more advanced RDI is said to be a parallel to the Hughes units fitted to America's top-line fighters, the McDonnell Douglas F-15 Eagle and F-18 Hornet. Unfortunately RDI has been a long time in the making, so that it will now be June 1986 before it can take over from the RDMs fitted in early production Mirage 2000s.

It will also be 1986 before French models of the aircraft get their definitive mark of SNECMA M53 engine, the -P2. Initial models of this turbofan (or, more accurately, continuous-bleed turbojet) were designated M53-2, the type completing its 150-hour bench test at Saclay in April 1976 at a rating of 8,500kg (18,739lb) thrust, with reheat. The M53-5 took this to 9,000kg (19,840lb), whereas the -P2 (first known as the -7) will have a bypass ratio of 0.4, a new fan and low-pressure compressor to increase power to 9,700kg (21,385lb). Dry rating

of this modular engine in its -P2 form will be 6,580kg (14,505lb), though the AA will retain about 160 M53-5s (including spares) in their original condition and not buy update modules for them.

Funding of three prototypes had increased to cover four and a Dassault-sponsored example by the time the project was a year old, and in the remarkable interval of only 27 months the prototype was flying — and beautifully, at that. Built at St Cloud, No 01 was assembled at Istres, where it made its initial flight on 10 March 1978. In a 65min sortie No 01 achieved Mach 1.02 at 36,000ft on the 5,500kg (12,125lb) dry thrust of its M53-2 before test pilot Jean Coureau selected afterburner to rise to 40,000ft and Mach 1.3. At that time the M53 had flown some 500 hours in the Caravelle (since 18 July 1973) and another 189 in the Mirage F1 M53, excluding bench testing. In a dozen more flights, taking up to the end of May,

Below:
As the result of early trials, Mirage 2000 No 01 was modified, both with wing trailing edge fillets extended rearwards almost to the afterburner nozzle, and a shorter fin.

Top:

The first two Mirage 2000 prototypes prepare for the day's flying.

Above:

Mirage 2000 No 02 in the original configuration. Note the leading edge flaps deployed for slow-speed control.

the aircraft had reached Mach 2 and an indicated airspeed of 1,205km/hr (749mph).

Such is the present nature of air fighting that these figure are merely of academic interest — a throwback to earlier decades, when 'How fast does it go?' was the first question to be asked about any new fighter. Everyone knew by now that Dassault could make an aeroplane exceed Mach 2; of far more significance was how *slowly* it would fly and whether it possessed high agility. Within a short time 2000-01 was showing an approach speed of 260km/hr (162mph) and landing speed of 232km/hr (144mph), further demonstrating an airspeed of 204km/hr (127mph) at 26° incidence, still under excellent lateral control.

If any had lingering doubts on the performance advantages of the CCV, they were speedily dispelled at Farnborough that September when, with only some 60 hours on the clock, the prototype Mirage 2000 gave a scintillating performance of its agility in the hands of Guy Mitaux-Maurouard. Even more was to come in a series of 22 flights at Istres by Maurouard and

Jean-Marie Saget between November 1980 and March 1981 which resulted in the Mirage 2000 being cleared for all manoeuvres from 0 to 1,480km/hr (0 to 920mph). Carrying various combinations of missiles, bombs and tanks, No 01 was flown at airspeeds down to zero at differing attitudes, including angles of attack exceeding 90°. At the same time the airframe was cleared for load factors of 9g (after tests on static specimen No 06 at Toulouse) and, with up to four AAMs, a roll rate of 270°/sec throughout the flight envelope.

Assisting in the flight-test programme, the second prototype flew at Istres on 18 September 1978, making a 50min sortie with Mitaux-Maurouard in command, and was seen to have a taller, narrower fin than its predecessor. Powered by an M53-5, its first tasks were carriage and separation of external stores and trials of the SFENA digital autopilot. Dummy missile drops included the first MATRA 550 Magic on 9 March

Above:
Trial launch of a MATRA Super 530 from the starboard pylon of Mirage 2000 No 02.

Below:
A more purposeful camouflage colour scheme is worn by Mirage 2000 No 04, together with an IFR probe, Super 530 and Magic AAMs.

1981 and first Super 530F on 27 July, the aircraft also proving its ability to operate with 1,700litre (374gal) underwing tanks and engage an airfield arrester wire at 297km/hr (176mph) at a weight of 16,000kg (35,275lb). Unfortunately, on 9 May 1984 No 02 became the first Mirage 2000 to be destroyed in an accident, after power was lost on the approach to Istres and test pilot Saget safely ejected from 250ft. No blame attached to the aircraft itself, for contaminated fuel was found to be the reason (after it had claimed a Jaguar from the base two days later).

Fitted with a full weapons system and nine strongpoints, No 03 was first taken aloft on 26 April 1979, and by the middle of the next month the three prototypes had flown 167 hours in 179 sorties and been sampled by 12 pilots. No 03 became the first with an RDM radar, on 13 November 1980, also finding time to conduct flight-refuelling experiments with a C-135F tanker during the following autumn. Since then it has been used for weapon system trials, including the Super 530 AAM. Last of the officially-funded aircraft, but first to production (Mirage 2000C) standard, No 04 flew from Istres on 12 May 1980 with a full weapons system and had a shorter, wider chord tailfin with less curvature, plus revised fairings at the intersection of the wing trailing edge and fuselage. Having joined No 03 in tanker trials, it has been operated from Istres testing the ECM system.

The two-seat Mirage 2000B prototype, B01, also had the full weapons system, and as such it first flew at Istres on 11 October 1980, Michael Porta achieving Mach 1.3 at 40,000ft and increasing flights by the five trials aircraft to 660. It flew 18 hours and 20 sorties during its first month at the start of precision testing of the FBW system. Early in 1981 B01 became the second fitted with an RDM radar, going on to conduct compatibility trials with the Aérospatiale ASMP nuclear

Above:

Fitted with a full weapon system, the first Mirage 2000B trainer flew at Istres on 11 October 1980 and later participated in refuelling trials. It carries under the wing an RP62 tank of 1,300 litre (286gal) capacity.

stand-off weapon and act as a trials vehicle for the export Mirage 2000. Naturally, it has been a most useful demonstration aircraft for foreign pilots wishing to handle the Mirage 2000 and report back to their governments.

First opportunities for the AA to make a detailed assessment of the aircraft which was taking 43% of its equipment budget by 1979 was early in the following year. All three then flying underwent official trials at the CEV, during which (in May) they pushed total time past 500 hours and devoted six sorties to the CEAM. After this successful test, No 01 continued its airframe and flight controls trials, then went to SNECMA, fitted with an M53-5 engine. The definitive M53-P2, which began bench running in 1982 and passed its 50-hour test in February 1983, was first taken into the air by No 01 on 1 July 1983.

As described later, even without its intended radar and optimum mark of engine, the Mirage 2000C entered squadron service two years after the target set by Gen Saint-Cricq. On that basis the AA might still have been waiting for the more complex Mirage G8 — or even the ACF — but taking a realistic view, two years' under-estimate is not bad for an aircraft such as the 2000. If it continues to work 'as advertised', living up to early promise, it will form France's first line of air defence and a vital component of the nuclear deterrent force. So Mirage 2000s will undertake roles presently assigned to Mirage IVAs, Mirage F1s and some Mirage IIIs, all three of their predecessors. Perhaps in this case the over-worked epithet 'Super Mirage' might be applied without fear of exaggeration.

In three ranks, the 12 Mirage 2000s taxied purposefully towards the VIPs and assembled guests, having just touched-down for the first time on their new home airfield. Wearing the historic stork insignia of the famous 'Cigognes' squadron, the aircraft drew to a halt, to be welcomed into service by M Charles Hernu, the French Defence Minister, and Gen Bernard Capillon, Chief of Staff of the Armée de l'Air. On 2 July 1984 — exactly 50 years to the day that the French Air Force was officially established as an independent armed service — the initial Mirage 2000 squadron was formed.

The AA had long been preparing for this moment, though first it had to be voted the funds to acquire the aircraft. Events got off to a bad start in 1979, the first year of procurement, when a mere four of the requested 20 Mirage 2000s were authorised. The target was 127 to be funded in the 1977-82 planning period, but things became worse, not better, in its final three years when 22, 22 and 25 were included in the defence budgets instead of the requested 23, 43 and 44. Furthermore, there had been a change of government in 1981, and consternation resulted in political and military circles during parliamentary debates of the next year's plans when it emerged that the new administration had made retrospective cuts in the 1982 cash allocations. All the last 25 Mirage 2000s were cancelled — as were the final 21 Mirage F1s, which had been bought specifically to make up for delays in the 2000 programme by maintaining front-line strength.

It is expected that home orders for Mirage 2000s will eventually amount to over 200 interceptors and some 100 nuclear strike 2000N versions (described later in this chapter). The present and

Below:
7 June 1982: the fuselage of the first production Mirage 2000C is taken from the line at Argenteuil for transfer to the final assembly plant at Bordeaux.

projected order situation up to the end of the 1984-88 plan is thus:

	Mirage 2000B	Mirage 2000C	Mirage 2000N
1979	—	4	—
1980	4	18	—
1981	7	15	—
1982	—	—	—
1983	6	9	15
1984	2	10	16
1985	2	10	16
1986-88*	} 71		38
Totals		158	85

*planned

Deliveries have been planned as eight 2000B/Cs in 1983, 70 in 1984-88, and 80 after 1988; plus 36 2000Ns in 1984-88, and 49 after 1988, making a grand total of 243, excluding prototypes.

As usual, assembly of production aircraft is taking place at Bordeaux-Mérignac. It was to here that the first 2000C fuselage was taken by road from Argenteuil, Paris, on 7 June 1982, to be mated to wings from Dassault's Martignas plant, near Bordeaux, and a fin from Aérospatiale at Nantes. Like the first 50 or so production aircraft, No C1 was fitted with a Thomson-CSF RDM radar and a SNECMA M53-5 powerplant, before Guy Mitaux-Maurouard took it for its first flight on 20 November 1982. It has been retained at Istres for armament system integration trials, including firing missiles and cannon, whilst No C2 (flown on 21 January 1983) later discarded its −5 engine to emerge as only the second fitted with a definitive M53-P2.

Below:
The fourth production Mirage 2000C was painted in the markings of EC 1/2 'Cigognes' late in 1983 for publicity purposes, although assigned to the CEAM for development.

It was therefore No C3 which became the first to join the AA when it was delivered to the CEAM at Mont-de-Marsan soon after its maiden flight on 15 March 1983. Wearing the code group 118-AV and the blue and grey upper surface camouflage adopted by production aircraft, it was displayed statically in the Defence Pavillion at that year's Paris Air Show. Other early production aircraft also went to the CEAM, of which No 4 was the first to be marked in the insignia of 'Cigognes', coded '2-EA', late in 1983, though it subsequently returned to development work as 118-AW. By the end of the first year, aircraft up to No C7 (14 December) had flown, as had the initial trainer, No B501, on 7 October.

B501 is important to the future success of the Mirage 2000C interceptor, for it has been retained at Brétigny-sur-Orge, near Paris, as a development aircraft fitted with RDI radar — the proposed standard fit. Accordingly No B502 (flown on 11 January 1984) became the first trainer to enter AA service when it was delivered to the CEAM as 118-AZ. Not included in the main production numbering sequence were two further development Mirage 2000Cs which were assembled at Istres late in 1983 and early in the following year. These are assigned to long-term research, and one, numbered X7, made its public debut at the 1984 Hannover Air Show.

Had the Mirage 2000C programme — and specifically its intercept-optimised RDI radar — been on schedule, re-equipment of the entire French Air Defence Command (Commandement Air des Forces de Défense Aérienne — CAFDA) would have begun with replacement of the ageing Mirage IIICs of the 10 Escadre de Chasse at Creil. However, when it became apparent that early aircraft would have to be fitted with the multi-mode RDM radar, plans were changed and EC 2 became the premier unit. Based at Dijon-Longvic, the 2nd Fighter Wing previously operated two squadrons of Mirage IIIEs in the tactical air superiority and ground-attack role, plus an OCU, and so the first step was to transfer it from the Tactical Air Force (FATac) to CAFDA on 1 July 1983.

Above:
Officially the first aircraft for EC 1/2, Mirage 2000C No 7 first flew on 14 December 1983 and was formally accepted by the squadron on 2 July 1984.

One of the three component squadrons, Escadron de Chasse 1/2 'Cigognes', stood down on 23 December 1983 and 18 of its pilots and 91 maintenance personnel were posted to Mont-de-Marsan in April 1984 to familiarise themselves with the Mirage 2000C. For pilots the course lasted nine weeks, the first three devoted to ground study at the Ensemble Mobile d'Instruction Mirage 2000, a travelling technical instruction unit which had formed at Rochefort (the AA's main technical school) as far back as February 1978. For the next six weeks pilots converted to the 2000C in some 30 sorties including circuits, low-altitude navigation, instrument flying, aerobatics, combat, use of radar, air-to-air firing and night flying.

This procedure was a temporary measure and has been replaced by one of two courses, dependent upon personnel experience. Established fighter pilots now transition in courses involving 10 sorties, 10 hours in a simulator and four hours in the DAISY (Dispositif d'Animation d'Images Synthétiques) nav/attack system trainer. DAISY was delivered to Mont-de-Marsan in 1983 and is a simulator for the head-up and head-down system employed in the Mirage 2000C, though initially it was optimised for the Mirage F1. (Two other DAISYs will be produced for Dassault's flight-test department and another has been ordered by Peru.) The full Mirage 2000C simulator, a three-axis unit, was delivered to Dijon early in 1985. For those coming straight from flying school after advanced instruction and general weapons training on the Alpha Jet, the Mirage 2000C conversion course is increased to 15 simulator hours and six on the DAISY in addition to flying.

The first squadron pilots to be converted flew eight 2000Cs and four 2000Bs (some of them on loan from Mont-de-Marsan) to Dijon on 2 July 1984. As the initial equipment of EC 2, this will be used to train pilots for the two remaining squadrons in the 2nd wing: EC 3/2 'Alsace', which becomes operational in 1985, and EC 2/2 'Côte

d'Or', late in 1986. The latter will keep its OCU role by taking charge of the two-seat 2000Bs formerly operated by its predecessors, and it may also receive the first few 2000Cs fitted with the keenly-awaited RDI radar — though only for the purpose of converting later squadrons. As Gen Capillon remarked at the acceptance ceremony, 'We can do a lot with the Mirage 2000 fitted with RDM and the M53-5, but we are looking forward to receiving Mirages with the greater-thrust −P2 and the RDI'.

No official information has been released concerning the other CAFDA units to be equipped with Mirage 2000B/Cs, yet it may be presumed that nine more squadrons will pass their Mirage F1s to FATac (as Mirage IIIE replacements) in order to operate the balance of the 200 or so to be procured. Those involved will be EC 5 at Orange, EC 12 at Cambrai and ECTT 30 at Reims the last-mentioned increased to three squadrons in 1985 when EC 10 disbanded at Creil.

As first delivered to the AA, Mirage 2000Cs have been armed with MATRA 550 Magic infra-red AAMs and radar-guided Super 530Fs, pending service clearances for the all-aspect Magic 2 and MATRA's Doppler-optimised Super 530D. In a series of 20 Magic 1 firings conducted before the end of 1983, three involved No C1 launching live rounds at an Aérospatiale CT.20 drone, one with the aircraft at the maximum stabilised flight angle of 29°. A further 20 Super 530 launches and dummy drops were executed in the same time-scale, including eight with the definitive Super 530D. The first full-scale test of a Super 530D took place against a CT.20 drone flying at Mach 2 over the Biscarosse weapons range on 26 October 1984, and made full use of the 530D's

Carrying a Magic AAM training round on the outer wing pylons, 2000C No 9 is '2-ED' of EC 1/2.

height differential capability. A weapons development agreement signed by Dassault and MATRA in November 1983 covers a two-year period and calls for a total of 100 launches of the Magic 2 and Super 530D, plus 200 proving flights of ground-attack armament: 1,000kg (2,205lb) laser-guided bombs, the new ARMAT anti-radiation missile, Durandal anti-runway bomblet dispensers, Beluga grenade launchers, rocket pods and retarded bombs. This comprehensive plan should satisfy most potential users, though it covers only part of the large variety of weaponry which the aircraft may carry.

Supplementary armaments include a podded DEFA 30mm cannon, with 300 rounds, first carried for trials by No B01. The pod allows 2000Bs to make up for their lack of internal cannon, though AA interest in the weapon seems to be for boosting the fire-power of Mirage IIIEs and F1s. (Incidentally, it is worth recording here that in addition to having the accepted longer fuselage, the trainer features a further 5in/13cm of wing-span compared with the 2000C.) Another weapon fitment undertaken on a trial basis has been of two Aérospatiale AS-30L ASMs, plus an associated Thomson PDL (Pod de Designation Laser).

In parallel with this development effort for France's new interceptor, Dassault was working on a very different Mirage 2000 variant. The cancelled ACF of 1975 was to have carried the Aérospatiale ASMP nuclear missile, and so it came as little surprise when two prototypes of a strike-optimised Mirage 2000 were authorised in 1979. First known as the Mirage 2000P (for Pénétration), then 2000N (Nucléaire), the prototype was flown at Istres for 65min by Michel Porta on 3 February 1983, achieving Mach 1.5. Its second sortie, on the following day, was the 2,000th by a Mirage 2000, whilst on the fifth flight it carried an observer in the rear seat for the first time. Wearing green and grey camouflage, No N01 was exhibited at the 1983 Paris Salon and joined in the air by a companion on 21 September of the same year — Porta again conducting the initial flight.

Though the tandem cockpit prompts comparison with a 2000B trainer, the 2000N differs in many subtle respects. Most importantly its airframe is strengthened to withstand the stresses of flight at up to 1,100km/hr (685mph) at a mere 200ft (61m) above the ground, and the two-man crew is provided with a comprehensive suite of avionics. In addition to 'special' ECM protection, this includes Antilope V terrain-following radar in the nose (replacing RDM/RDI), two SAGEM ULISS

Mirage 2000 weapon load options.

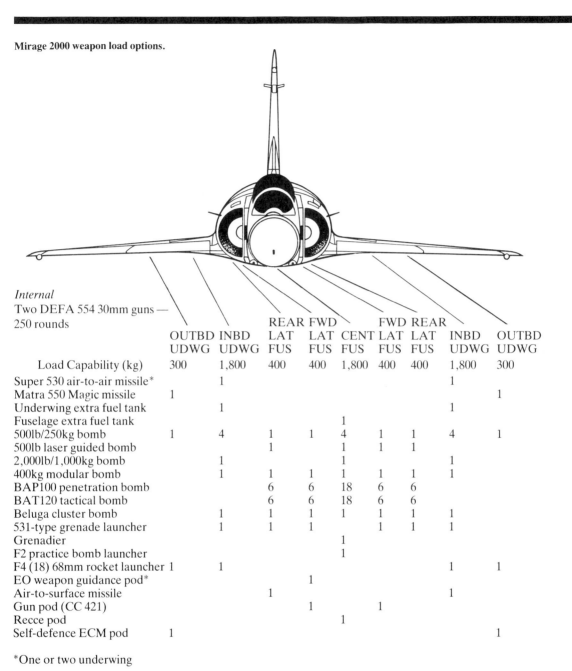

Internal
Two DEFA 554 30mm guns — 250 rounds

	OUTBD UDWG	INBD UDWG	REAR LAT FUS	FWD LAT FUS	CENT FUS	FWD LAT FUS	REAR LAT FUS	INBD UDWG	OUTBD UDWG
Load Capability (kg)	300	1,800	400	400	1,800	400	400	1,800	300
Super 530 air-to-air missile*		1						1	
Matra 550 Magic missile	1								1
Underwing extra fuel tank		1						1	
Fuselage extra fuel tank					1				
500lb/250kg bomb	1	4	1	1	4	1	1	4	1
500lb laser guided bomb		1			1	1	1		
2,000lb/1,000kg bomb	1				1			1	
400kg modular bomb	1		1	1	1	1	1	1	
BAP100 penetration bomb			6	6	18	6	6		
BAT120 tactical bomb			6	6	18	6	6		
Beluga cluster bomb	1		1	1	1	1	1	1	
531-type grenade launcher	1		1	1		1	1	1	
Grenadier					1				
F2 practice bomb launcher					1				
F4 (18) 68mm rocket launcher	1	1						1	1
EO weapon guidance pod*				1					
Air-to-surface missile			1					1	
Gun pod (CC 421)				1		1			
Recce pod					1				
Self-defence ECM pod	1								1

*One or two underwing

52 inertial platforms, an improved TRT AHV 12 altimeter, Thomason-CSF colour TV displays, and an OMERA vertical camera. By early 1984 the prototypes were flying automatically below 300ft in development trials, supported by the additional efforts of a Falcon 20 operating from the CEV, Bretigny, with a 2000N weapons system installed.

Both 2000N prototypes have M53-5 engines, though when series aircraft are supplied in 1986 they will be the first in the AA with uprated −P2 powerplants. Available from March 1985, the −P2 was first fitted to export Mirage 2000s for India, and though a −5 can be brought up to the higher standard by replacement of three modules, it is believed that the AA will retain −5s in early 2000B/Cs.

Some re-allocation of inter-departmental responsibilities will accompany the Mirage 2000N's entry to AA service, for it will operate with the Tactical Air Force (FATac) whilst also replacing the Mirage IVAs of Strategic Air Command (FAS). In practice it is to provide a stand-off capability for FATac's two nuclear strike wings: EC 4 with Mirage IIIEs and EC 7 with Jaguars, both presently armed with free-fall AN 52 nuclear bombs. Five 2000N squadrons will form at the rate of one per year from 1988 onwards, starting with the two components of EC 4 at Luxeuil (EC 1/4 'Dauphine' and EC 2/4 'Lafayette'). Between 1990 and 1992 the Jaguar squadrons expected to convert, are EC 1/7 'Provence' and EC 3/7 'Languedoc', both at St Dizier, and EC 4/7 'Limousin' at Istres (leaving EC 2/7 'Argonne', the Jaguar OCU).

France's commitment to the Mirage 2000 may be seen to be as great as the RAF investment in the Panavia Tornado as the prime weapon for both strike and air superiority. In view of its critical importance to French defence, the Mirage 2000 *must* be effective in both roles. The air force is convinced that it will be, though realises that a complex weapon system requires careful assimilation. Fittingly, therefore, the last word goes to Gen Capillon, from his welcoming speech for the aircraft at Dijon in July 1984 (when the opportunity was not lost to make a forceful appeal for additional funding): 'There is still a lot which remains to be done — or should I say, remains to be *given* — to allow us to . . . proceed properly with the programme'. France will undoubtedly lead the way, but five other countries will be close behind.

Below:
No 4 made a second attempt to impersonate an aircraft of EC 1/2 during the commissioning ceremony in July 1984. It was one of several trials aircraft painted in squadron markings as part of a move to disguise the shortage of production deliveries at that time.

Bottom:
First production Mirage 2000B trainer, No 501 is assigned to trials of the RDI radar, but masqueraded as an aircraft of EC 1/2 during the unit's commissioning in July 1984.

Dassault Moves Up-Market

Such is Dassault's reputation for combat aircraft design that strong overseas interest was being shown in the Mirage 2000 whilst it was still a prototype and four countries had ordered 104 examples even before EC 1/2's stork insignia had been painted on the fin of a production aircraft. Although earlier successes with the Mirage III/5 and F1 would make such information appear as 'dog bites man' news, closer analysis of the situation reveals a different position.

By 1982 it was possible to buy a new Mirage III/5 or F1 for $9-10million 'fly away' (that is to say, without spares, training and technical support), when a General Dynamics F-16 Fighting Falcon would be priced at $16million in the same condition, and Northrop was offering F-20A Tigersharks at $10.3million. With the advent of the Mirage 2000, however, Dassault was no longer able to undercut the market. Priced at some $20million per copy and needing perhaps the same

amount in support, the new French Fighter was no longer the automatic choice of countries requiring an inexpensive, simple, proven fighter. The Mirage 2000 is an advanced aircraft with control systems, construction methods and avionics to match, and it faces strong competition from the US — and Soviet — aircraft industries.

What do customers get for their money? In brief, a multi-role fighter-bomber, at home in the air defence role or carrying a combination of ground attack ordnance and fuel tanks on its four

Below:
In close formation are three Mirage 2000 prototypes and (at the rear) the sole Mirage 4000. No 01 is leading, with No 02 on the starboard flank and No 03 to port. The two last-mentioned were without the extended trailing edge fillets when this photograph was taken.

wing and five fuselage strongpoints. All export aircraft are equipped with the Thomson-CSF RDM Export multi-mode radar (AA aircraft have the slightly different RDM France) which includes an illuminator for semi-active radar-homing AAMs — the MATRA Super 530D being the obvious choice. These missiles would be mounted on the inboard wing pylons, with a MATRA 550 Magic infra-red homing AAM outboard though Magic can occupy all four positions if the operational situation so demands. For attack (as examplified by the Mirage 2000N) the external load is up to 6,000kg (13,225lb) of bombs, rockets and missiles. The Aérospatiale ASMP, of course, is not for sale.

Structurally, the Mirage 2000 comprises a semi-monocoque fuselage with 'area rule' waisting allied to a multi-spar wing of 58° sweepback. For manoeuvrability and a minimum stable flight speed of a very creditable 167km/hr (104mph), the wing is equipped with a full-span automatic leading-edge flaps which operate in unison with two-section elevons extending the entire length of the trailing edge. Leading-edge flaps automatically retract to reduce drag during acceleration and low-altitude cruise, but act with the trailing-edge units to provide variable camber during combat. A fly-by-wire control system operates elevons, flaps and rudder, with movement provided by two 4,000lb/sq in hydraulic systems.

Hydraulic power is also required for movement of the Messier-Hispano-Bugatti undercarriage, in which single mainwheels retract inward and the twin-wheel nose unit retracts rearward. The latter is steerable through 45° each side of centre, whilst on landing the aircraft may use an airfield arrestor hook or the brake parachute installed in a fairing above the jet nozzle. Electrical power is supplied from two Auxilec 20kVA 400Hz constant frequency alternators. There is a retractable in-flight refuelling probe fitted on the starboard side of the fuselage, ahead of the windscreen.

The pilot, who (in a Mirage 2000C) occupies a Martin-Baker F10Q zero-zero ejection seat in an air-conditioned, pressurised cockpit, is assisted by a comprehensive avionics suite including RDM radar, a single SAGEM ULISS 52 inertial platform, ESD central digital computer, Thomson-CSF VE-130 head-up and VMC-180 head-down displays, SFENA 605 autopilot, Thomson-CSF/ESD electronic countermeasures equipment, MATRA Spirale passive countermeasures, LMT Deltac TACAN and IFF transponder, TRT radio altimeter and a Thomson-CSF laser designator and marked target seeker.

Performance details include a maximum continuous speed of Mach 2.2 (1,482km/hr or 921mph IAS), but more realistically the aircraft will fly at 1,110km/hr (690mph) low level, without after-

burning, and carrying a load of eight 250kg (550lb) bombs and two Magic AAMs. Its range in this configuration is over 1,480km (920 miles). In clean condition it has an initial climb rate of 15,000m/min (49,200ft/min) and will actually reach 15,000m, flying at Mach 2, in just 4min. Using radar-homing missiles, the Mirage 2000 can destroy a Mach 3 intruder flying at 80,000ft in less than 5min from brakes off, though its service ceiling is only 59,000ft.

Five nations other than France had bought Mirage 2000s at the time of writing, and brief details of their procurement are given below.

Abu Dhabi Requiring 36 replacements for its Mirage III/5s as the basis of an expanded air defence network, the ADAF ordered an initial 18 aircraft on 16 May 1983, these to be delivered in 1986 with M53-P2 engines. At the same time options were taken on a similar quantity with 1987-88 delivery dates, the complete order to be worth some $1,500million including spares, support and training, if this were exercised. The ADAF contract covers 12 Mirage 2000EADs, three 2000RAD reconnaissance models (the first of this sub-type ordered) and three 2000DAD trainers. In January 1985 it was reported that Abu Dhabi had confirmed purchase of the second 18 Mirage 2000s, payment to be made in the form of 15million barrels of oil, and had taken an option on a third batch of 18. Each batch includes five spare engines.

Egypt The initial Mirage 2000 overseas customer, Egypt ordered 20 aircraft worth $890million in January 1982 from a requirement for between 60 and 80. As part of the offset arrangements, the Arab Organisation for Industrialisation aircraft plant (Factory 36) at Helwan secured six million man-hours of work from Dassault, including production of at least 10% of components for its first 20 Mirage 2000s. Delivery of these (16 Mirage 2000EMs and four 2000BM trainers) will begin late in 1985 after pilot training at Mont-de-Marsan. A repeat batch of 20 aircraft was ordered in 1984 for assembly at Helwan from CKD (completely knocked-down) kits.

Greece For political reasons the Greek competition for new fighters has been split between two types of European aircraft and two from the US. In August 1984, whilst the General Dynamics F-16 and McDonnell Douglas F-18 were still in competition, the Greek Government announced that it had elected to buy 40 Mirage 2000s in preference to Panavia Tornados for the European part of the programme. Originally the Greek Air Force (but not necessarily its Government masters) had shied away from Dassault because of complaints about the cost and delivery of spares for its Mirage F1s. The position was eased by the award to Hellenic Aerospace Industries early in 1984 of 'exclusive world rights to Mirage F1 general repairs and spare parts manufacture'. Late in 1984, Greece also announced that it would purchase 40 General Dynamics F-16 Fighting Falcons and take options on a further 20 Mirage 2000s and 20 F-16s — only one of which would be exercised, in about 1987-88.

India Though previously associated with Dassault through its earlier operation of Ouragans

and Mystère IVAs, the Bharatiya Vayu Sena did not become a Mirage customer until a Memorandum of Understanding (MoU) was signed on 24 January 1982 covering 40 aircraft and provision for later assembly of CKD kits and, eventually, licensed production. The first part of this MoU was confirmed in October 1982 when 36 Mirage 2000Hs and four 2000TH trainers were ordered for delivery between October 1984 and December 1986. Because of production delays, the first Mirage 2000H did not make its initial flight until 21 September 1984, resulting in a two-month postponement of IAF pilot training in France. No 225 Squadron formed in 1985 with personnel trained by the manufacturer, and a second unit was earmarked for formation in India before the end of the same year. The four trainers and first 26 fighters have M53-5 engines, but these will be retro-fitted with M53-P2s at a later stage, the IAF being the initial operator of the -P2 engine.

Below:
Showing-off its slow-speed handling characteristics, Mirage 2000 No 04 keeps pace with a Robin light aircraft.

Armament will include MATRA Super 530D and Magic 2 AAMs.

India made no secret of the fact that its Mirage 2000s were bought to counter the purchase of 40 F-16 Fighting Falcons by its neighbour, Pakistan. Plans for additional acquisitions beyond parity involved 40 CKD kits and 70 to be built with an increased local content by Hindustan Aeronautics Ltd. During negotiations the proportion varied, first to 45+65, then 20+90, the latter scheme to take two and seven years respectively. France offered to assist with transferring to India the advanced technology associated with manufacturing the aircraft, but interest in the scheme waned as the Soviet Union offered MiG-31 'Foxhounds' and MiG-29 'Fulcrums' at artificially low prices. The local assembly option expired in summer 1984, though unconfirmed reports suggest one or two more squadrons of Mirage 2000s may be ordered directly from France.

Peru Ironically, in view of Indian intentions outlined above, Peru decided to obtain Mirage 2000s because it was dissatisfied with the Soviet-supplied Sukhoi Su-22 'Fitters' which it operates in three squadrons. At first, in 1982, interest was shown in 26 F-16/79s (Fighting Falcons with a lower-power J79 engine), this changing after a visit to Lima by French Defence Minister Charles Hernu in September 1982. On 15 December that year a $700million Letter of Intent was signed for two batches of aircraft: 14 Mirage 2000Ps and two

2000DP trainers, followed at a later, unspecified date by a further eight and two respectively. These are claimed by Dassault as a definite order for 26 aircraft. During 1983 Peruvian financial problems and a Soviet offer of MiG-23 'Floggers' for air defence prompted reports that the LoI would be cancelled. However, a firm order was reported to have been signed early in 1984, calling for the first to be handed-over in January 1985.

Delivery of export aircraft is being undertaken in parallel with Mirage 2000s for home use, production being due to build up from two per month at the beginning of 1984 to seven by late 1986. Deliveries to all customers during 1984 were

Above left:
A Mirage 2000C pictured from the boom operator's position of a Boeing C-135F tanker.

Above
India's first Mirage 2000H flew at Bordeaux on 21 September 1984. France provided training facilities for the IAF before deliveries began in 1985.

Left:
Weapon options for the Mirage 2000.

planned to total 27, followed by 53 in 1985. The fabrication cycle (from the first nut and bolt to completed aircraft) is 22 months, or 24 months for a two-seat aircraft.

With the exception of the recent Greek commitment, no Mirage 2000s have been ordered by European air forces. This omission is not due to neglect on Dassault's part, for early in 1978 it was offering a radically modified variant known as the Mirage 3000 to nearby air arms. The prime feature of the 3000 was use of *two* Turbo Union RB.199 turbofans (as in the Tornado). Each is rated at over 7,660kg (16,000lb) thrust, or slightly less than an M53, so the Mirage 3000's performance is better imagined than described. Of course, the Mirage 3000 itself existed only in the imagination of Dassault's design team, because there were no takers.

Now the St Cloud designers are again working on an aircraft which could be a true European fighter, accepted by all the West's major air forces. Until recently without a name, it deserves mention because it is a recognisable member of the Mirage family. Logically, it can be described together with the latest 'Big Mirage' which nobody appears to want: the Mirage 4000.

5 The Mirage 4000 and Into the Future

Mirage Magic

The seasoned Paris airshow regulars take much in their stride, but even they felt compelled to crane their necks with the rest of the crowd as Jean-Marie Saget put the big, twin-engined delta through its paces — it was not that the Mirage 4000 drowned out conversation (though that was certainly a secondary factor), but the ease with which such a large aircraft of that configuration could perform slow-speed, high-angle-of-attack flypasts. With a mere 20 hours of flying behind it, the prototype Mirage 4000 was giving a convincing display of its potential at the 1979 Salon de l'Aéronautique. Observers were convinced that the French Government could not ignore yet another star performer from the Dassault stable and would purchase Mirage 4000s as replacements for the Mirage IVA. They were wrong.

What was first known as the Delta Super Mirage was revealed in December 1975 — the very moment that the ACF was being terminated. Suitable for long-range interdiction and interception, it was at first billed as an export aircraft, this apparently being confirmed when the mock-up was revealed in November 1977 to the accompaniment of hints that Saudi Arabia was funding the development programme. The reports persisted, and late in 1980 the Saudi Defence Minister, Prince Sultan Ibn Abdul Aziz, went as far as to announce in public that procurement was being considered. An unofficial report at the same time claimed that Saudi Arabia had already given Dassault FFr4,000million (about $800million) in progress payments and was thinking in terms of an initial batch of 24. However, at the time of writing — four years later — the Mirage 4000 continues to wait for customers and has slipped from the limelight.

Funded with private capital, the single Mirage 4000 prototype was scheduled to fly in October 1978, although it was 9 March 1979 before Jean-Marie Saget took off from Istres for a one-hour maiden flight. Powered by two SNECMA M53-2s, No 01 achieved Mach 1.2 and an altitude of 36,000ft, solely under the control of its fly-by-wire system. Making rapid progress the aircraft flew at Mach 1.6 on its second sortie three days later, and then was briefly grounded for the usual inspections after a third flight on 13 March. During two sorties late in March Mach 1.5 was flown at the take-off weight of around 20 tonnes (44,000lb), and on flight 6 (11 April) Saget reached Mach 2.04 at 35,000ft. In the last-mentioned flight, which lasted 75min, the aircraft demonstrated its ability to fly at a 25° angle of attack and made an initial exploration of aerobatic capabilities.

By the end of 1979 the prototype had amassed 72 hours in 52 sorties and had been flown under control down to 231km/hr (144mph). The following spring saw it carrying immense 2,500litre (550gal) under-wing tanks and receiving the strongest expression yet of local interest. A leaked report by the defence committee of what was then the ruling political party in France proposed allocating FFr23,000million ($5,600million) for a fleet of 50 Mirage 4000s to follow on from the Mirage IVA. The report was significant, even

Below:
The Mirage 4000 prototype flew for the first time on 9 March 1979, piloted by Jean-Marie Saget.

Above:

Finished in an overall white colour scheme, the Mirage 4000 has thrilled the air display crowds with its fine control at low speed, but potential customers have failed to be impressed.

though not a Government document, and Defence Minister Yvon Bourges fuelled speculation by stating officially that it was not possible to say at that time whether or not France would buy the aircraft.

Ever hopeful, the Mirage 4000 ended 1980 with some 100 hours to its credit, flown by five pilots: three Dassault, one CEV and one from the Armée de l'Air. In mid-1981, after 150 hours, it had completed the basic flight-test programme and was ready to be fitted with a Mirage 2000 navigation and attack system (but with a larger 80cm antenna for improved radar range). It also changed to the initial production M53-5 engines by the time of the 1981 Paris Salon, and again demonstrated the agility stemming from a thrust : weight ratio well in excess of unity. At the 1982 Farnborough display No 01 flew in interceptor and ground-attack configurations on alternate days, using all 12 attachment points (six beneath the fuselage) in the latter instance. These held two 2,500litre tanks, two Sycamor ECM pods, two MATRA Magic AAMs, a laser designator pod, two AS-30L ASMs, two 1,000kg (2,200lb) laser-guided bombs and an EMD Antilope terrain-following radar pod.

As an interceptor the Mirage 4000 will achieve speeds in excess of Mach 2.3 and reach 50,000ft at Mach 2 just 3min after brakes off. Its ceiling is 65,000ft, and range with external tanks is in the region of 3,700km (2,300miles). Such impressive figures prompted the Dassault company (51% State-owned since 1981) to announce plans for construction of a second aircraft which would be to the projected operational standard. This has yet to appear.

Now overshadowing the Mirage 4000 is Dassault's efforts to secure a major share in the European Fighter Aircraft (EFA) programme. Defined in broad terms by the air staffs of Britain, France, West Germany, Italy and Spain in December 1983, the EFA will have a ready-made market for almost 900, and may be expected to secure export orders. After some false starts, the EFA — dubbed 'Eurofighter' — emerged in response to parallel studies conducted by the aircraft industries of France, Germany and Britain, and it was agreed that 'technology demonstrator' aircraft should be produced by those with sufficient interest and capital.

Even before the penta-national agreement, Dassault had announced (in June 1982) its intention of designing an advanced aircraft, the fore-runner of which would be known as the Avion de Combat Expérimental (ACX). This was to be equipped with such new systems as SNECMA M88 turbofans, Thomson-CSF RACAAS radar and MATRA MICA air-to-air missiles, and it received government approval late in 1982, followed on 13 April 1983 by authorisation to build a demonstrator to make its first flight in 1986. In view of its tight schedule, the prototype will be powered by two General Electric F404 turbofans of some 7,260kg (16,000lb) thrust each, and the M88 will continue as a separate programme for later incorporation in production aircraft. French aims are for the definitive aircraft to replace the Armée de l'Air's Jaguars (the Avion de Combat Tactique 95 requirement) and Aéronavale Super Etendards from about 1995 onwards. This will mean production of some 200 ACTs and 80 ACMs — the latter indicating Avion de Combat Marine. Early in 1985 the ACX prototype was christened 'Le Rafale' which translates into English (rather uninspiringly) as 'squall'.

Main guidelines in the design have been high manoeuvrability, steep angles of attack (AoA) in

117

flight, and short take-off and landing. Dassault has retained the well-tried delta in the ACX, but with the addition of augmented span and compound sweep, as well as a large-area, all-moving canard surface linked with the digital fly-by-wire control system. Semi-ventral air intakes will ensure the engines receive adequate air at high AoAs. The new concept of voice command (a simple version of which has been flying in a Mirage IIIR at CEV Brétigny since July 1982) for some systems will be included, and the automatic computer-controlled flight system is to have provision for anti-turbulence ride control for low-level operations. Efforts will be made to reduce the ACX's radar signature through use of 'absorbant' materials and

aerodynamic techniques, and more than half the airframe will be built of composite materials, leaving only the centre fuselage to be made of metal. Estimates quote an empty weight of about 10 tonnes (22,000lb) and a maximum take-off weight, without external stores, of 15 tonnes (33,000lb).

The ACX mock-up was revealed at the 1983 Paris Salon where, by accident or design, it was displayed a few feet from another wooden aircraft of similar concept projected by British Aerospace. The proximity was illusory, for strong national wills on both sides of the Channel make it appear that neither country will subject itself to an EFA programme in which the other has design leadership, even though, ideally, the EFA should combine the best of all projects. However, it could be that the French aircraft will be perpetuated as a unilateral project if it fails to form the basis of the Eurofighter. Should France have the resources to persevere with the ACX and its derivatives, one may predict with some certainty that when it enters the front line its designation will include the legendary synonym for excellence in combat aircraft: *Mirage*.

Appendices

1 Dassault Mirage Production

Listed below are details of Mirage production, including those aircraft built under licence — and Mirage 'cousins' produced in Israel. In the latter case it will be seen that aircraft serial numbers are deliberately misleading in the IDF/AF, being issued (and probably re-issued) at random. Totals in the 'quantity' column, where given in parentheses, will be found to refer to conversions or transfers originally listed elsewhere. Aircraft are for French use unless otherwise stated, those with numbers beginning 01 being trials aircraft which are not normally included in sales totals. French and other operators' serial numbers are given in the remarks column, and it should be noted in this connection that French constructor's numbers are by no means always used as serial numbers.

Mirage III

Variant	Quantity	Remarks
Mirage I	1	No 01
Mirage III	1	No 001 (converted to Balzac V No 001)
Mirage IIIA	10	Nos 01-010
Mirage IIIB	28	Nos 01, 201-227 (No 225 converted to IIIB-SV)
Mirage IIIB-1	5	Nos 231-235
Mirage IIIB-2	10	Nos 241-250, also known as Mirage IIIB-RV
Mirage IIIBE	20	Nos 257-276 (Nos 257, 258 and 265 to Saudi/Egypt 2001-2003; Nos 271 and 272 to Argentina I-021 and I-021 — sequence unknown; one assigned to Chile, 1984)
Mirage IIIBJ	5	Israel: 287, 618, 639, 769 and 789 (c/n 236-240, sequence unknown except 639 is c/n 237; survivors to Argentina C-720 to C-722 including C-721 c/n 237.
Mirage IIIBL	2	Lebanon: L511 and 512 (c/n 251 and 252)
Mirage IIIBS	4	Switzerland: U-2001 to U-2004
Mirage IIIBZ	3	South Africa: 816-818 (c/n 228-230)
Mirage IIIC	95	Nos 1-95
Mirage IIIC-2	(1)	See IIIE No 406
Mirage IIICJ	72	Israel: random serials including 02, 08, 11, 14, 34, 44, 45, 52, 67, 82, 103, 111, 147, 148, 150, 151, 153, 158, 159, 171, 176, 178, 180, 296, 406, 409, 459, 507, 522, 524, 534, 620, 649, 703, 712, 719, 720, 725, 729, 730, 732, 741, 743, 749, 753, 755, 756, 758, 764, 768, 771, 775, 776, 779, 780, 833, 915, 941, 942, 948, 951, 952 (c/ns 101-148, 152, 154-156, 159, 160, 162, 165-167, 169, 170, 173, 174, 176, 177, 179, 180, 182-187). Survivors to Argentina as C-701 to C-719
Mirage IIICS	1	Switzerland: J-2201 (c/n 96)
Mirage IIICZ	16	South Africa: 800-815 (c/n 149-151, 153, 157, 158, 161, 163, 164, 168, 171, 172, 175)
Mirage IIID	16	Australia: A3-101 to A3-116
Mirage IIIDA	2	Argentina: I-001 and I-002
Mirage IIIDBR	6	Brazil: 4900-4903 (c/n 253-256); 4904 and 4905

Mirage IIIDE	6	Spain: CE.11-1 to CE.11-6, reserialled CE.11-25 to CE.11-30
Mirage IIIDP	5	Pakistan: 67.301-67.303, 70.304 and 70.305
Mirage IIIDS	2	Switzerland: J-2011 and J-2012
Mirage IIIDZ	3	South Africa: 839-841
Mirage IIID2Z	11	South Africa: 843-853
Mirage IIIE	192	Nos 01-03, 401-408, 410, 412, 414, 415, 417-419, 421-440, 443, 445, 447, 449, 451-458, 460-463, 465-531, 533-535, 537-539, 541, 545-579, 583-590, 605-625 (Nos 557-559 to Saudi/Egypt 1001-1003; No 589 to Milan S-01, later Mirage 50 No 01, later Mirage 3NG No 01; No 406 later Mirage IIIC2)
Mirage IIIEA	17	Argentina: I-003 to I-019
Mirage IIIEBR	16	Brazil: 4910-4925
Mirage IIIEE	24	Spain: C.11-1 to C.11-24
Mirage IIIEL	10	Lebanon: L501-510
Mirage IIIEP	18	Pakistan: 67.101-67.106 (c/n 532, 536, 540, 542-544 — sequence uncertain), 67.107-67.118
Mirage IIIEV	10	Venezuela: eg 0624, 1207, 2483, 7162, 7381, 8940
Mirage IIIEZ	17	South Africa: 819-834 (c/n 435, 437, 441, 442, 444, 446, 448, 450. 409, 411, 459, 413, 465, 416, 464, 420). 842
Mirage 3NG	(1)	No 01 (ex-Mirage 50 No 01)
Mirage IIIO	(1)	Australia
Mirage IIIOA	50	Australia: A3-51 to A3-100
Mirage IIIOF	50	Australia: A3-1 to A3-50 (most later IIIOA)
Mirage IIIR	52	Nos 01 and 02, 301-350 (344 converted to Mirage Milan)
Mirage IIIRD	20	Nos 351-370
Mirage IIIRJ	(2)	Israel: 34 and 60 converted from IIICJ
Mirage IIIRP	13	Pakistan: 67.201-67.203 and 75.204-75.213
Mirage IIIRS	18	Switzerland: R-2101 to R-2118
Mirage IIIRZ	4	South Africa: 835-838
Mirage IIIR2Z	4	South Africa: 854-857
Mirage IIIS	36	Switzerland: J-2301 to J-2336
Mirage IIIT	1	No 01
Mirage IIIV	2	Nos 01 and 02
Mirage Milan	(1)	No 01 (ex-Mirage IIIR No 344)

Mirage IV

Mirage IVA	66	Nos 01-04 and 1 to 62
Mirage IVP	—	No 01 (ex-No 8), No 02, and 18 'production' conversions from IVA

Mirage 5

Mirage 5	1	No 01
Mirage 5AD	12	Abu Dhabi: 401-412
Mirage 5BA	63	Belgium: MA01-MA03 (later BA01-BA03), BA04-BA63. Allocated c/ns 01-63
Mirage 5BD:	16	Belgium: MD01-MD03 (later BD01-BD03), BD04-BD16. Allocated c/ns 201-216
Mirage 5BR	27	Belgium: BR01-BR27. Allocated c/ns 301-327
Mirage 5COA	14	Colombia: 3021-3034
Mirage 5COD	2	Colombia: 3001 and 3002
Mirage 5COR	2	Colombia: 3011 and 3012
Mirage 5D	53	Libya: 401-453
Mirage 5DAD	3	Abu Dhabi: 201-203
Mirage 5DD	15	Libya: 201-215
Mirage 5DE	32	Libya 101-132
Mirage 5DG	4	Gabon: 201-204
Mirage 5DM	3	Zaire: M201-M203
Mirage 5DP	5	Peru: 197-199 plus two
Mirage 5DP1		Peru: conversions
Mirage 5DP3		Peru: conversions

Mirage 5DPA2	2	Pakistan: 79.306 and 79. 307
Mirage 5DR	10	Libya: 301-310
Mirage 5DV	2	Venezuela: 5471 and 5472
Mirage 5EAD	14	Abu Dhabi: 501-514
Mirage 5E2	16	Egypt: 9161-9176 (requires confirmation)
Mirage 5F	58	Nos 1-50 (ex-Mirage 5J), Nos 51-58 (new)
Mirage 5G	3	Gabon: 401-403
Mirage 5G-II	(4)	Gabon: 501-504 ex-Libya
Mirage 5J	(50)	Israel. Diverted to Mirage 5F
Mirage 5M	14	Zaire: M401-M414
Mirage 5P	32	Peru: 182-195, 101-114, plus others. Ten to Argentina in June 1982 and reserialled, including C-403, C-407, C-409, C-410, C-419, C-428, C-430 and C-439.
Mirage 5P3		Peru: conversions
Mirage 5P4		Peru: conversions
Mirage 5PA	28	Pakistan: 70.401-70.428
Mirage 5PA2/3	30	Pakistan: 79.429-79.458
Mirage 5RAD	3	Abu Dhabi: 601-603
Mirage 5SDD	3(3)	Egypt (Saudi Arabia): 2001-2003 (ex IIIBE Nos 257, 258 and 265), 2004-2006
Mirage 5SDE	29 (3)	Egypt (Saudi Arabia): 1001-1003 (ex IIIE Nos 557-559), 1004-1032. Reserialled in 9101 range
Mirage 5SDR	6	Egypt: 3001-3006
Mirage 5SSE	22	Egypt: 1033-1054. Reserialled in 9101 range
Mirage 5V	4	Venezuela: 1297, 2473, 7162 and 9510

Mirage 50

Mirage 50	—	No 01 (ex-Milan S-01; to Mirage 3NG No 01)
Mirage 50FC	(8)	Chile: 501-508 (ex-Mirage 5F Nos 1, 3, 5, 8, 16, 23, 28 and 30, sequence unknown)
Mirage 50C	6	Chile: 509-514
Mirage 50DC	2	Chile: 515 and 516
Mirage Milan S	—	No 01 (ex-Mirage IIIE No 589; to Mirage 50 No 1)

IAI Nesher and Dagger

Nesher	50?	Israel, eg 501, 524-527, 533, 534, 562, 565, 566, 586, 598, 599
Nesher T	6+	Israeli serials unknown; reportedly built from French kits
Dagger	(36)	Argentina: between C-401 and C-437 ex-Nesher
Nesher T	(3)	Argentina: C-426, C-438 c/n T-04 and C-439 c/n T-07

IAI Kfir

Kfir		Israel, eg 703, 705, 706, 707*, 709, 710*, 711, 712*, 714*, 716*, 718*, 719, 724, 725*, 726, 727, 730-740, 742*, 743*, 745, 749*, 750, 755*, 759*, 761, 764, 779*, 781, 786*, 787* (*indicates conversion to Kfir C2).
Kfir C2		eg 805, 807, 812-814, 821, 822, 824, 826, 827, 829-831, 837, 838, 841, 845, 846, 849, 851, 853-855, 857, 858, 860, 862, 864-866, 868, 870-872, 877-880, 882-885, 887, 891, 894, 895, 897, 928, 948, 961, 979, 987, 988
Kfir TC2		Israel, eg 303, 304, 306, 611
Kfir C7		Israel, conversions from C2, eg 824, 895

Mirage G

Mirage G	1	No 01
Mirage G8	2	Nos 01 and 02

Mirage F1

Mirage F1	4	Nos 01-04
Mirage F1AD-200	16	Libya: 401-416

Mirage F1AZ	32	South Africa 216-247
Mirage F1B	20	Nos 501-520
Mirage F1BD	6	Libya: 201-206
Mirage F1BE	6	Spain: CE.14-26 to CE.14-31
Mirage F1BJ	2	Jordan: 2518 and 2519
Mirage F1BK	3	Kuwait: 771 and 772 (reserialled 719 and 720) plus one
Mirage F1BQ	16	Iraq: 4000-4005, 4500-4505, 4556 and 4557, probably 4558 and 4559 (last two batches with IFR probes)
Mirage F1C	83	Nos 1-50, 52, 54, 55, 58, 60, 62-64, 67-85, 87, 90, 100-103. (Nos 1 and 11 converted to F1C-200 and reserialled Nos 201 and 224)
Mirage F1C-200	81	Nos 201 and 224 (converted from F1Cs Nos 1 and 11); Nos 202-204 and 208 (pre-delivery conversion of F1Cs Nos 92, 95, 98 and 99); Nos 205-207, 209-223, 225-283
Mirage F1CE	45	Spain: C.14-1 to C.14-25, C.14-32 to C.14-51
Mirage F1CG	40	Greece: 101-116 (ex-F1C Nos 51, 53, 56, 57, 59, 61, 65, 66, 86, 88, 89, 91, 93, 94, 96, 97, sequence unknown), 117-140
Mirage F1CH	25	Morocco: 126-150
Mirage F1CJ	17	Jordan: 2501-2517
Mirage F1CK	30	Kuwait: 701-718, plus 12
Mirage F1CR-200	43	Nos 601 and 602 (ex-Nos 01 and 02), Nos 603-643
Mirage F1CZ	18	South Africa: 200-215, 203 (No 2), 204 (No 2)
Mirage F1DDA	2	Qatar: QA-61 and QA-62
Mirage F1E	(1)	No 01
Mirage F1ED	16	Libya: 501-516 (527-541 also reported)
Mirage F1EDA	12	Qatar: QA-71 to QA-81
Mirage F1EE-200	22	Spain: C.14-52 to C.14-73
Mirage F1EH-200	25	Morocco: 151-175
Mirage F1EJ	27	Jordan: 101-117 plus 10
Mirage F1EQ	30	Iraq: 4006-4035
Mirage F1EQ-200	23	Iraq: 4506-4528
Mirage F1EQ5-200	20	Iraq: beginning 4560
Mirage F1JA	16	Ecuador: 801-816
Mirage F1JE	2	Ecuador: 830 and 831

Mirage F2

Mirage F2	(1)	No 01

Mirage 2000

Mirage 2000	4	Nos 01-04
Mirage 2000B	20	Nos B-01, 501-519
Mirage 2000BM	8	Egypt
Mirage 2000C	56	Nos 1-56 (139 planned up to 1988)
Mirage 2000DAD	3	Abu Dhabi
Mirage 2000DP	4	Peru, including 193
Mirage 2000EAD	12	Abu Dhabi
Mirage 2000EM	32	Egypt
Mirage 2000H	36	India: KF101-KF136
Mirage 2000N	33	Nos N-01, N-02, 1-31 (87 planned up to 1988)
Mirage 2000P	22	Peru
Mirage 2000RAD	3	Abu Dhabi
Mirage 2000TH	4	India: KT201-204
Mirage 2000	40	Greece

Mirage 4000

Mirage 4000	1	No 01

ACX

ACX/Rafale	1	No 01 (under construction)

2 Mirage Squadrons of l'Armee de l'Air

The squadrons detailed below operate, have operated or will operate one or more variants of the Dassault-Breguet Mirage family. Information quoted for each comprises the unit's designation, name, base, parent command, fin insignia (left side first unless otherwise stated) and brief notes on aircraft usage. Mirage IVAs do not normally carry unit insignia.

EC 1/2 'Cigognes' Dijon, CAFDA. SPA 3 (stork, wings downwards); SPA 103 (stork, wings raised). Mirage IIIC first delivery 10 July 1961 (Mirage IIIB 1963-66). 10,000 flying hours September 1964; 15,000 hours January 1966. Conversion to IIIE begun at CEAM April 1968. Last IIIC withdrawn 1 October 1968. Re-equipped with IIIE. Transferred from FATac to CAFDA on 1 July 1983. Stood-down 23 December 1983 for Mirage 2000 conversion at CEAM from April 1984. Officially received 2000C 2 July 1984.

ECT 2/2 'Côte d'or' Dijon, CAFDA. Two insignia from SPA 57 (seamew), SPA (chimera) and SPA 94 (grim reaper). Formed 1 April 1965 as EC 2/2 with Mirage IIIB and IIIC with only SPA 65. Added SPA 57 in June 1965. Redesignated ECT 2/2 31 October 1968. First IIIBE received 14 April 1971. Added SPA 94 6 October 1972. Mirage IIIC withdrawn 1978. Mirage IIIR added in May 1983. Transferred from FATac to CAFDA on 1 July 1983. Trained first Spanish pilots from 6 March 1970; Libyan from 16 June 1970; Lebanese 12 January 1971; Colombian 26 November 1971; Argentine 1972; Brazilian June 1982; Venezuelan 1973; Saudi/Egyptian early-1974; Zairose July 1974; Chilean 1979. Expected to pass Mirage III OCU task to EC 1/13 and re-equip with Mirage 2000B in 1986.

EC 3/2 'Alsace' Dijon, CAFDA. Both sides: Alsace arms. Received first Mirage IIIC 12 December 1961 (Mirage IIIB early-1963 to early-1966). Aircraft withdrawn 5 April 1968. First IIIE delivered 27 September 1968. Transferred from FATac to CAFDA on 1 July 1983. To receive Mirage 2000C 1985.

EC 1/3 'Navarre' Nancy, FATac. SPA 95 (pennant), SPA 153 (lammergeyer). First Mirage IIIE sortie 2 May 1966. Based at Lahr, West Germany, until September 1967.

EC 2/3 'Champagne' Nancy, FATac. SPA 67 (stork), SPA 75 (falcon). Began training 15 September 1965. First Mirage IIIE received (at Colmar) 17 January 1966. Based at Lahr, West Germany, until September 1967.

EC 3/3 'Ardennes' Nancy, FATac. Both sides: a boar's head. Formed with Mirage 5F 1 July 1974, following delivery of first aircraft on 5 June 1974. Converted to Jaguar in February 1977 and aircraft to EC 2/13.

EC 1/4 'Dauphine' Luxeuil, FATac. SPA 37 (condor), SPA 81 (greyhound). First Mirage IIIE sortie 1 February 1967. To re-equip with Mirage 2000N in 1988.

EC 2/4 'Lafayette' Luxeuil, FATac. N 124 (Sioux head), SPA 167 (stork). Crew training begun (with EC 3 at Lahr) 15 April 1966. First Mirage IIIE received 14 October 1966. Will convert to Mirage 2000N in 1989.

EC 1/5 'Vendeé' Orange, CAFDA. SPA 124 (Joan of Arc), SPA 26 (stork). Crew training begun at Dijon April 1966. First Mirage IIIC sortie 19 July 1966. Officially re-equipped 1 September 1966. First six Mirage F1Cs received at Orange 21 March 1975.

EC 2/5 'Ile de France' Orange, CAFDA. Both sides: Ile de France arms. Crew training begun at Dijon October 1966. Received first Mirage IIICs 7 November 1966. Converted to Mirage F1C from June 1975 and withdrew last IIIC 17 November 1975. (EC 5 made first Mirage F1C-200 in-flight refuelling sortie 9 February 1978.)

EC 3/5 'Comtat Venaissin' Orange, CAFDA. SPA 171 (dragon), ERC 571 (pirate pennant). Formed 1 April 1981 and commissioned 3 July 1981 with Mirage F1B (and three F1Cs).

123

EC 1/7 'Provence' St Dizier, FATac. SPA 15 (knight's helmet)' SPA 77 (Jerusalem cross). Current with SEPECAT Jaguar. To receive Mirage 2000N in 1988.

EC 2/7 'Argonne' St Dizier, FATac. SPA 31 (Spartan archer), SPA 48 (cockerel). Current with SEPECAT Jaguar. To receive Mirage 2000N in 1989.

EC 3/7 'Languedoc' St Dizier FATac. SPA 38 (thistle), 3C-1 (shark). Current with SEPECAT Jaguar. To receive Mirage 2000N in 1990.

EC 1/10 'Valois' Creil, CAFDA. SPA 93 (goose), N84 (fox's mask). Received first Mirage IIIC 1 August 1974. Converted to Mirage F1 from May 1981. Transferred to ECTT 30 at Reims in 1985.

EC 2/10 'Seine' Creil, CAFDA. Both sides: GC II/10-3e (Cercle de Chasse de Paris). Operational with Mirage IIIC 9 December 1968. Disbanded 1985.

EC 3/10 'Vexin' Djibouti, CAFDA. Both sides: GC III/10 (musketeer). Formed at Creil 1 September 1978. Commissioned at Djibouti 1 January 1979 with 10 Mirage IIICs. Expected to be renumbered EC 4/2.

EC 1/12 'Cambresis' Cambrai, CAFDA. SPA 89 (hornet), SPA 192 (tiger's face.) Began crew training for Mirage F1C April 1977 and discarded last Super Mystère B2 9 September 1977.

EC 2/12 'Picardie' Cambrai, CAFDA. SPA 172 (parrot), SPA 173 (bluebird). Formed with Mirage F1 1 June 1980.

EC 3/12 'Cornouailles' Cambrai, CAFDA. Bulldog's head and scorpion. Crew training for Mirage F1C begun at Reims (ECTT 30) early-1976. First aircraft to Cambrai 1 October 1976. Designated EC 2/12 until 1 June 1979.

EC 1/13 'Artois' Colmar, FATac. SPA 100 (swallow), SPA 83 (chimera). Received Mirage IIIC from 13 March 1962. Converted to Mirage IIIE 1-30 June 1965. Expected to assume OCU role as ECT 1/13 with Mirage IIIB/BE from ECT 2/2.

EC 2/13 'Alpes' Colmar, FATac. Both sides: a mounted knight. Received first Mirage IIIC 29 May 1962 (Mirage IIIB June 1964 to June 1966). Re-equipped with Mirage IIIE 1 April

1965. Re-equipped with Mirage 5F (from EC 3/3) February 1977.

EC 3/13 'Auvergne' Colmar, FATac. SPA 85 (jester), GC II/9-4e (sword and shield). Formed with Mirage 5F 1 May 1972 after first delivery on 5 April 1972.

ECTT 1/30 'Loire' Reims, CAFDA. Both sides: C 46 (trident). Formed 1985 from EC 1/10.

ECTT 2/30 'Normandie-Niemen' Reims, CAFDA. Both sides: Normandy badge. Crew training at CEAM by EC 24/118 1973. First Mirage F1 delivered to Creil 20 December 1973. Operational 5 July 1974.

ECTT 3/30 'Lorraine' Reims, CAFDA. Both sides: Lorraine badge. Converted to Mirage F1 1974.

ER 1/33 'Belfort' Strasbourg, FATac. Both sides: SAL 33 (battleaxe). Converted to Mirage IIIR 1967.

ER 2/33 'Savoie' Strasbourg, FATac. Both sides: SAL 6 (seamew). Received first Mirage IIIRs January 1964. Conversion to Mirage F1CR begun April 1983. First aircraft to Strasbourg on 1 July 1983 and formally entered service on 7 September 1983.

ER 3/33 'Moselle' Strasbourg, FATac. Both sides: BR 11 (paper hen). Received Mirage IIIBs for training from 18 March 1963. First Mirage IIIR received 7 June 1963. Converted to IIIRD (first received 1 April 1968).

EB 1/91 'Gascogne' Mont-de-Marsan, CoFAS. Formed 1 October 1964 with Mirage IVA. To receive Mirage IVP in 1986.

EB 2/91 'Bretagne' Cazaux, FAS. Formed 1 December 1965 with Mirage IVA. To receive Mirage IVP in 1986.

EB 3/91 'Cévennes' Orange, FAS. Formed as EB 2/93 on 29 March 1965 with Mirage IVA. Redesignated EB 3/91 on 1 July 1976. Disbanded 1 October 1983.

EB 1/94 'Guyenne' Avord, FAS Formed as EB 1/93 at Istres on 5 February 1965 with Mirage IVA. Disbanded 10 June 1976. Re-formed at Avord 1 July 1976, again operating Mirage IVAs.

EB 2/94 'Marne' St Dizier, FAS. Formed as EB 2/94 on 1 October 1965 with Mirage IVA.

EB 3/94 'Arbois' Luxeuil, FAS. Formed with Mirage IVA on 1 February 1966. Disbanded 1983.

EB 'Beauvaisis' Creil, FAS. Formed with Mirage IVA as EB 3/91. Disbanded 1 July 1976.

EB 'Sambre' Cambrai, FAS. Formed with Mirage IVA as EB 3/93. Disbanded 1 July 1976.

EB 'Bourbonnais' Avord, FAS. Formed with Mirage IVA as EB 1/94. Disbanded 1 July 1976.

EC 24/118 (CEAM) Mont-de-Marsan, CAFDA. Both sides: a human figure within a triangle. Has operated all types of Mirage at various times.

ERI 1/328 (CIFAS) Bordeaux, FAS. Formed with Mirage IVA.

EE 2/328 (CIFAS) Bordeaux, FAS. Both sides: an eagle. Formed with Mirage IIIB/IIIB-RV.

Key to abbreviations

CAFDA	Commandement Air des Forces de Défense Aérienne
FATac	Force Aérienne Tactique
CEAM	Centre d'Expérimentations Aériennes Militaires
FAS	Forces Aériennes Stratégiques
EB	Escadron de Bombardement
EC	Escadron de Chasse
ECT	Escadron de Chasse et de Transformation
ECTT	Escadron de Chasse Tous Temps
EE	Escadron d'Entrainement
ER	Escadron de Reconnaissance
ERI	Escadron de Reconnaissance et de Instruction

Above:
The ageing Mirage IV will remain a potent weapon well into the next decade following addition of Aérospatiale ASMP nuclear stand-off bombs to 18 of the type. A programme of ASMP trial launches was almost complete by the middle of 1985.

Above:
American Mirage. The United States Navy's VF-43 squadron at Oceana, Virginia, took delivery of the first of 12 IAI Kfir C2s on 29 April 1985 for 'aggressor' training. Despite its new designation, F-21A, and low-visibility blue-grey camouflage, the aircraft is still recognisable as a member of the Mirage family.

Below:
Iraq has used its Mirage F1EQ5-200s, with their Aérospatiale AM.39 Exocet missiles, for anti-shipping attacks in the Gulf. The first attempted combat mission, on 3 December 1984, ended in failure because of interface problems between missile and aircraft, but the combination was operational by late-February 1985.

Above:
Mirage 2000N No 01 is the first of two prototypes of the nuclear strike model. An ASMP nuclear stand-off weapon on the centreline pylon is largely concealed by a fuel tank and self-defence MATRA Magic AAM.

Below:
By the spring of 1985, when its major components had been brought together at St Cloud's experimental shop, the Dassault ACX demonstrator had been named the 'Rafale' (squall). In the event of France going ahead alone with a new fighter programme, it will be difficult to resist returning to the traditional name of Mirage for the production version. The Rafale's first flight is due in June 1986.

	Mirage I	Mirage IIIB	Mirage IIIC	Mirage IIIE
Engine	2 × MD30R	Atar 9B-3	Atar 9B-3	Atar 9C-3
dry (lb st)	2 × 1,642	9,460	9,460	9,430
a/burning (lb st)	2 × 2,160	13,225	13,225	13,225
Rocket type	SEPR 66	SEPR 841	SEPR 841	SEPR 844
Thrust (lb)	3,370	3,370	3,370	3,370
Span	23ft 2in	27ft 0in	27ft 0in	27ft 0in
Length	35ft 9in	50ft 6in	48ft 6in	49ft 4in
Height	11ft 6in	14ft 9in	14ft 9in	14ft 9in
Wing area (sq ft)	200	377	377	377
Empty weight (lb)	8,000	13,820	13,040	15,540
Max TOW (lb)	11,905	26,455	26,015	30,200
Max speed (Mach)	1.3	n/a	2.15	2.2
Combat radius (miles)	n/a	n/a	745	745

	Mirage IIIR	Mirage 5	Mirage 50	Mirage 3NG	Milan S
Engine	Atar 9C-3	Atar 9C-3	Atar 9K50	Atar 9K50	Atar 9K50
dry (lb st)	9,430	9,430	11,055	11,055	11,055
a/burning (lb st)	13,230	13,230	15,873	15,873	15,873
Rocket type	SEPR 844	SEPR 844	SEPR 844	SEPR 844	SEPR 844
thrust (lb)	3,370	3,370	3,370	3,370	3,370
Span	27ft 0in	27ft 0in	27ft 0in	27ft 0in	27ft 0in
Length	50ft 10in	51ft 0in	51ft 0in	51ft 4in	51ft 9in
Height	14ft 9in	14ft 9in	14ft 9in	14ft 9in	14ft 9in
Wing area (sq ft)	377	377	377	377	377
Empty weight (lb)	14,550	14,550	15,765	15,540	15,540
Max TOW (lb)	30,200	30,200	31,000	32,400	30,864
Max speed (Mach)	n/a	2.2	2.2	2.2	2.2
Combat radius (miles)	n/a	800	400	n/a	n/a

	Mirage IV	Mirage F1	Mirage 2000C	Mirage 4000	ACX
Engine	2 × Atar 9K	Atar 9K50	M53-5	2 × M53-P2	n/a
dry (lb st)	10,350	11,055	12,350	14,500	n/a
a/burning	14,770	15,873	19,840	21,400	c1,6000
Rocket type	JATO	—	—	—	—
thrust (lb)	n/a	—	—	—	—
Span	38ft 11in	27ft 7in	29ft 6in (a)	39ft 5in	c37ft 0in
Length	77ft 1in	50ft 3in	47ft 7in (b)	61ft 4in	c52ft
Height	18ft 7in	14ft 9in	n/a	n/a	n/a
Wing area (ft)	840	269	441	786	n/a
Empty weight (lb)	31,965	16,315	n/a	n/a	n/a
Max TOW (lb)	69,665	35,715	36,375	n/a	n/a
Max speed (Mach)	2.2	2.2	2.3+	2.30	c2.0
Combat radius (miles)	n/a	n/a	n/a	1,150+	n/a

(a) 29ft 11in on Mirage 2000B
(b) 47ft 9in on Mirage 2000B

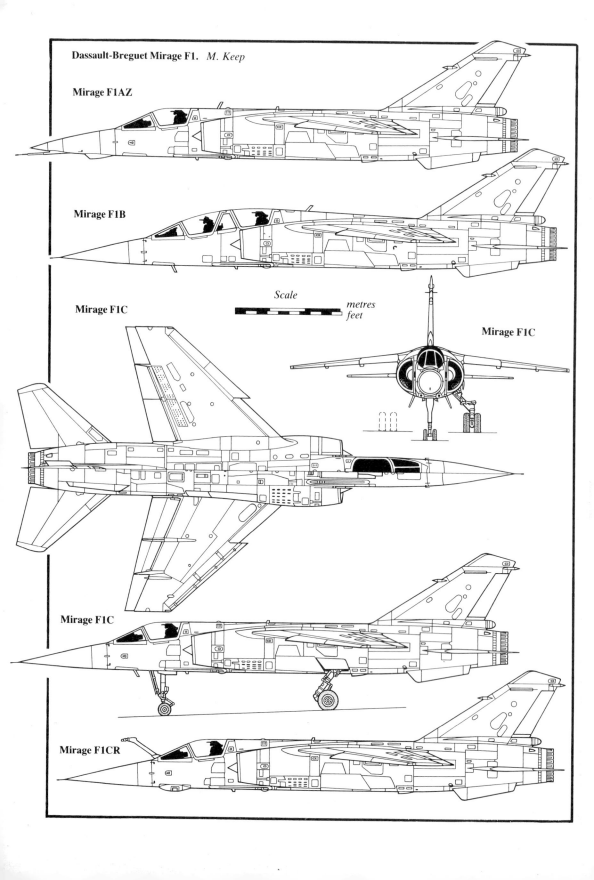

Dassault-Breguet Mirage F1. *M. Keep*

Mirage F1AZ

Mirage F1B

Mirage F1C

Scale

metres
feet

Mirage F1C

Mirage F1C

Mirage F1CR